Deeply Rooted

A personal and inspirational true-life story of overcoming
tragic deaths, infertility, miscarriages, lawsuits,
bankruptcy, and surrendering our dream home
with Jesus Christ

Kristi Lee Seymour

Trilogy Christian Publishers
A Wholly Owned Subsidary of Trinity Broadcasting Network
2442 Michelle Drive
Tustin, CA 92780

For information, address Trilogy Christian Publishing
Rights Department, 2442 Michelle Drive, Tustin, Ca 92780.
Trilogy Christian Publishing/ TBN and colophon are trademarks of Trinity Broadcasting Network.

For information about special discounts for bulk purchases, please contact Trilogy Christian Publishing.

Manufactured in the United States of America

10 9 8 7 6 5 4 3 2 1

Library of Congress Cataloging-in-Publication Data is available.

ISBN 978-1-64773-340-7 (Print Book)
ISBN 978-1-64773-341-4 (ebook)

With love to Jesus Christ, my Savior, my Healer, and my Friend.
Thanks for loving me first.

If I could speak all the languages of earth and of angels, but didn't love others, I would only be a noisy gong or a clanging cymbal. If I had the gift of prophecy, and if I understood all of God's secret plans and possessed all knowledge, and If I had such faith that I could move mountains, but didn't love others, I would be nothing. If I gave everything I have to the poor and even sacrificed my body, I could boast about it, but if I didn't love others, I would have gained nothing.

—1 Corinthians 13:1–3 NLT

Contents

acknowledgments

With deep appreciation:

To my honey, thank you for your faithfulness all these years. Without you, my life would have been boring! I love your sense of adventure and fearless approach to life. Thank you for always working so hard. Nothing ever came easy! You helped me fulfill the dream to stay home with our children. Thank you for your support and allowing me to share our story. You know I'd follow you anywhere! I love you!

To Little Herbie, my son (my monkey), our first miracle! You make me very proud! I know God has a calling on your life; you were born a natural leader! You bless me daily. I love you!

To Benjamin, my son (my bulldog), a pleasant surprise to both of us! You are a joy! You can do anything you put your mind to! I love your compassion for others. You are a mighty warrior of God! I love you!

To Joey, my son (my Jofish), you completed our family! I love your heart, your strength, and your spirit! You are thoughtful and very smart! May you follow God's path all your days! I love you!

Exodus and Justice, thanks for your prayers to the Father. We look forward to meeting you both!

To my mom, thank you for loving me. I always knew you did, even when times were hard. I appreciate your fighting spirit! I got that from you! I'm so thankful we get to spend eternity together. The devil didn't win! I love you!

To Mimi, thank you for not taking the advice of stepping in that mustard bath or allowing that doctor to terminate your pregnancy! Your oldest son was meant for me! Thank you for your support with my book and allowing me to share much of your story as well—our paths crossed a lot! I love and appreciate you!

To my twin, thank you, Keri, a.k.a. Mozzie, for all your insight and positive influence. I love our relationship! Thanks for all your prayers when I was a heathen!

To my brother Nathan and his wife, Kelli—thank you for your love and never missing a birthday!

To Stacy Baker from Trinity Broadcasting Network, thank you for believing in the first chapter of my book and saying yes to publish it!

To Pastor Dean and Terri, without you both, we might never have known Jesus! Thank you for your example and investing in two motley sheep! We love you both!

To John and Carol Cooper, thank you for speaking life to me! We appreciate your time, prayers, and investment in our dreams of becoming free! We're still believing!

To Leslie Howard, I'm so thankful God humbled me to get to know you. I admire the love you carry for Jesus and His wounded people. You are seated in heavenly places! May God fulfill your heart's desire!

To Sarah Oxman, what can I say? Thank you for inviting me and my family for dinner. This book may not have been if it wasn't for you and the life you spoke into me six months ago! Thank you for pushing me out of my comfort zone. May God bless you and your fearless family!

Last but certainly not least, prayer warriors! Thank you to the unseen faithful heroes who have gone to the front lines and battled on behalf of me and my loved ones. Whether God put us in your heart to pray, you called or texted us, or you responded to my request through church peeps at 2:00 a.m., I love being a part of the body of Christ! You all amaze me! May Jesus pour His abundant blessings on you!

Foreword

To my beautiful bride,

I'm so thankful for all these wonderful, crazy, complex years we've shared together! From hot-rod wallpaper (in our teens) to mango walls (in our forties) and everything in between.

I've been truly blessed to have you as my treasure. "The man who finds a wife finds a treasure and he receives favor from the Lord" (Proverbs 18:22 NLT).

You're more precious to me than rubies, my love. You're an amazing mother. I love watching you chase after our very energetic, competitive, strong-willed boys.

Thank you for loving my mom! It makes me laugh when I think about what the Lord must have been thinking when He created you, knowing He was going to give His daughter (you) to me. (I'm glad He didn't change His mind!)

This verse reminds me of you from Proverbs 31:10–12 NLT:

> Who can find a virtuous and capable wife? She is worth more precious than rubies. Her husband can trust her, and she will greatly enrich his life. She will not hinder him but help him all her life.

I love you, my wife, my friend.

Love always,
Your husband, *Herb*

Preface

Cause and Effect

I used to joke often with my honey (that's how I refer to my husband of twenty-three years) that one day I'm going to write a book about the crazy details in our life. There were so many times things happened to us that seemed strange or unusual. People wouldn't believe me when I told them! The Oxmans invited our family to a spaghetti-and-meatball dinner November 1, 2019 (their son has the same teacher as our oldest son). It took us almost two months to coincide schedules.

I became familiar with this hilarious family mainly through Facebook. Sometimes something special happens unexpectedly with complete strangers. We hit it off well. I'm not really much for small talk, so I opened up to Sarah about some of the details in this book. I was fascinated that she was a fearless living coach. I shared with her how I answered a Facebook ad from a Christian book publisher looking for authors. I told her I filled out the general information and noticed I had a couple of inquiries. I wanted to respond, but I was intimidated—not to mention I had a book *idea*, not an actual book yet. She was passionate when she urged me that I should respond. She said, "Kristi, what's the worst that can happen?"

"They say no?"

"What do you have to lose?"

She was right! She uplifted my spirits! I agreed at minimum I would respond and see what they had to say.

Two different people followed up with me. They were both males. I really felt strongly that if I was going to respond, I needed a female—and that's how I found Stacy! We had a telephone meeting, and she asked me how far I was on my book. I told her about half to three-quarters. She said, "Great! Send it to me!" Problem was, I only had the idea and an outline of the book in my handwriting journaled on notebooks.

I felt so overwhelmed. I e-mailed Stacy back and told her I wasn't able to give her what I originally wanted to, that this book had to come from God on His timing, not mine. You see, I didn't even know what a manuscript was! No, I'm not joking.

She kindly asked me if I could give her just one chapter; that seemed fair enough. Seven days later, I was signing my first agreement to publish my book! God works in mysterious ways!

This was my first year (after a decade of being a stay-at-home mom raising our three boys) that all three would be in school full-time. I had no idea God would call me to write this book when He did! If you think God's just going to clear a path and make things easy for you to do His will, think again! I thought I lost the files to my book once when my computer died out on me. I managed to save it to the cloud and didn't realize it till the next day (computers aren't my strength)! My twin sister almost died from a ruptured appendix, and as I wrote our story, the world went through a historic world-wide pandemic! My three boys, who were once in school, now I was homeschooling them on top of everything else! All to say, with God, all things are possible!

I'm so thankful for God's inspiration. I believe there's a divine anointing. Also, I'm so appreciative for that spaghetti-and-meatball dinner by the Oxmans! It gave me the boost I needed!

Our Dream Home Conceived

May he grant your heart's desires and make all your plans succeed.
May we shout for joy when we hear of your victory and raise a victory
banner in the name of our God. May the Lord answer all your prayers.

—Psalm 20:4–5 NLT

If you can picture two high school sweethearts walking together hand in hand past some old beat-up cars in the back of his mom and dad's thirty-eight-acre parcel of property, that was us. We walked past what once stood as a large beautiful barn, which was nothing other than a rubber roof and a makeshift three-bay garage. We certainly had vision. With squinted eyes and an outstretched arm, we would point to the eastern hilltop to the rear of the land that we believed would one day be called a home of our own.

If I'm not mistaken, it was the first day of sophomore year. We were instructed by our teacher to introduce ourselves to the class. I sat in the first row because my last name started with *B*. We were seated in alphabetical order. And as each of us were sharing our names, there was a boy in my class who proudly proclaimed his name as *Herb Seymour*. I can remember distinctly saying to myself, "I will *never* date a guy named Herb!" He had a medium husky build, with lines fashionably shaven into his sideburns. He was one of the few boys who was able to grow a mustache and was far from the blue-eyed blondes that I was attracted to.

During English class, we were assigned random partners by Mrs. Percier. It was one of those moments I'll never forget. I had a severe case of poison ivy that wreaked havoc on my face. It was so humiliating. I was self-conscious but quickly became even more

17

embarrassed when Herb was announced as my partner. I purposely kept my long brown hair down in hopes by some small effort I could conceal the awful red rash. As soon as Herb came and sat next to me, I was comforted by his compassion. He showed concern for me and suggested I keep my hair back away from my face and that it would only make the irritation worse. How sweet! The assignment we were given was poetry. I helped him write a poem to his girlfriend, Jaime. As I read his kind words to her, I found myself becoming interested in him. Let's just say my inner voice wanted him to break up with her so I would have a chance to be the one he would write to.

My twin sister, Keri, was the opposite of me. Our personalities were very different. I was the feminine one into hair and makeup, and she was the brut. Keri picked plant maintenance for her trade at Bay Path Regional Vocational Technical High School. She was interested in martial arts, heavy metal, and somewhat of an introvert. I wanted to be popular and picked fashion design as my vocation. As my crush on Herb grew, it became more obvious to my sister and younger brother, Nathan. We would walk almost a mile every day to the bus stop for school, and I would carelessly skip and sing corny songs I would make up about Herb.

Tina (one of my friends from shop) told me Herb was available. By this time, his girlfriend had broken off with him. I pretended to be sympathetic, but deep down, I was privately relishing the update. Keri knew of the affection I had for Herb and made it a point to threaten him. She told him if he didn't go "out" with me, she would beat him up. If you could believe, this really marked the beginning of our lifelong relationship as partners. I know it must sound strange, but it's true. The date was June 3, 1991. That was the day we began holding hands. I used to carry his books to class for him because he was on crutches from a sports injury. Keri could be very intimidating, even though she was no more than five feet tall, 120 pounds. She would arm-wrestle the football team for money during lunch and win. You can imagine how emasculated the guys must have felt.

Herb was quite a romantic guy. He used to shower me with flowers, candies, clothes, and would be the one to buy me my first car. He wrote me letters almost every day and would hand them to me in the hall between the sounding of the bell at school. That was our primary way of communicating. I was not allowed to date. I rarely would get the special privilege to call him. Eventually, my mom did give me a little leeway since Herb was so persistent. He remembered special occasions and was the guy who would spend fifty bucks to win me a five-dollar teddy bear at the Spencer County Fair. He truly did spoil me rotten, and I loved every minute of it too! He worked hard to earn money and spent most of it on me and his Buick. His trade of choice was auto body, but his dad convinced him plumbing could make a good living. Herb respected his dad's advice, so he chose the plumbing and heating trade. He made me feel beautiful, worthy, and smart. I used to help him with his homework a lot. He valued my opinion, and we were inseparable. We loved to go to the movies, out for dinner, or just spend time together with family. He was generous to a fault, full of energy, creative, and fearless.

Sometimes when he was spontaneous, it made me nervous. He had a beautiful blue 1966 Buick Special that he painted himself in his dad's garage. It sparkled radiantly in the sun. Uncle Tony and Aunt Joanie bought it for his sixteenth birthday. I loved the smell of the coconut air freshener he'd have dangling on his rear-view mirror. And I remember sticking to the black leather seats when I'd wear shorts in the summer. Herb was confident and had good manners. He was well liked by many and became popular. In high school, we were awarded with a few senior superlatives. Herb was voted Best Personality, Most Athletic, Most School Spirit, and we were elected Class Couple. He was the captain of the football and baseball team. I was flattered that they nominated me for Best Looking, but I struggled with that title for many reasons. First, I was still very insecure; and second, I had an identical twin sister. How can you name only one? It didn't feel right. Keri would laugh it off by saying I got the looks, but she got the brains.

Herb was an old-fashioned gentleman and would open the door for a lady. He did have some of his father's traits to a fault too. Herb would show moments of jealousy that I just passed off as cute until the time we went on a double date with friends. We were at a roller skating rink in Oxford, and there was another guy being flirty with me, flicking my hair as it flowed behind me while I was skating. I knew if he didn't leave me alone, it was going to get uncomfortable, so I warned him that I had a boyfriend, but it was too late. As were gliding down the rink, I looked over, and Herb had the guy by the neck with his skates dangling in the air against the wall. Needless to say, we had to leave and almost got into a fight we would have been outnumbered in. Life was good, at least for a little while.

I'm not entirely sure if I was even seventeen yet. I left home in a way I much regret today. I won't give much detail, but I left my mother, brother, and twin sister without any notice. All that remained was a bunch of childhood belongings and a shoebox of letters (which I hastily forgot) that captured years of hidden feelings I tried to keep from my mom. I envisioned myself sharing them later in my adult years with her, but I never intended for her to read them that way. It was the way I could vent my true emotions of anger and frustration. It was the way I could forgive and move on. I used the pen like a friendly therapist and purged all the hateful thoughts I would have about situations and people I was angry with.

My upbringing was difficult, and often I felt trapped. I went to live with an aunt and uncle for less than a year and, after a heated argument, found myself hopping in Herb's truck with most of my belongings. Herb told me he was going to give his parents an ultimatum: if they didn't take me in, we were going to get our own place even though we had no money and no idea of even where to begin. Nothing but the mercy of God covered us. I was so scared. I was on survival and, at this point, only thought of myself. It wasn't until later in my life I understood how abandoning the people I loved caused so much grief and rejection.

Herb's parents were gracious. I couldn't believe how hospitable they were. They made me feel welcome and part of the family. I was able to share a room with Herb (which surprised me), and their rules were far different from the ones I was used to abiding in. Herb's parents were foster parents, and it seemed like perfect chaos to me. Herb had two younger biological brothers, Keith and Sean. They were athletic and into football just like Herb was. Then there were four other foster children, a total of ten people including myself. With the occasional temporary placement for more children, there was always room for one more. I appreciated being treated like an adult. I got a job as a piece worker stitching popular labels onto T-shirts.

Herb's dad was named after his father, so that would make my boyfriend the third. Herbert Francis Seymour III. Doesn't that sound rich? Dad worked at a steel factory. He was a big guy who looked a little older than his real age. He was balding, had fair skin, the biggest blue eyes, smoked like a chimney, and drank lots of coffee. His belly laugh could have been mistaken for Santa Claus. He worked in the garage on old cars and hot rods with the boys. Oftentimes, Herb was the only one who could tolerate his orders. He wasn't the most patient man. But his bark was louder than his bite. They would do all kinds of things to make a little extra money. He didn't have a retirement, a pension, or money in the bank. They held on to old financial principles of not incurring a lot of debt and made use of what they had to make ends meet. Even though they were compensated through foster care, that hardly covered all the expenses of a large household.

Christmas Eve of the same year, we graduated high school. Herb knelt traditionally on one knee in his upstairs bedroom and asked me to marry him. I kind of chuckle now thinking back of how we were so young. His room that we were sharing at the time still had colorful wallpaper of tractor-trailer trucks and hot rods. We knew we wanted to be together. I wish I could say I was surprised, but I knew he was up to something because when I drove by the Auburn House of Diamonds Store, I noticed Herb's truck parked in the parking lot. I kind of ruined the surprise when I snooped inside to ask him what he was up to. He had been faithfully putting installments on a purchase he made of a beautiful 0.75 carat solitaire-diamond ring! There was no doubt in my heart he was the one I wanted to share forever with.

Herb's dad began to suffer from back pain. No one was prepared for the heartbreaking diagnosis of pancreatic cancer. He was only thirty-nine years old. We had suspicion that maybe whatever chemicals he was working with at the steel factory might have affected him, but we had no proof. Or was it caused by asbestos exposure on the ship when he served in the US Coast Guard? Everyone showed their own way of dealing with the shocking news; most of us were in denial. Family would often come by to visit more frequently than they used to. It was the first time we experienced a terminal illness with an immediate family member.

Herb sentimentally wanted to honor his dad with one last wish. He sold both of his trucks and came up with some cash to buy a bright-red 1965 Fastback Ford Mustang. It was a classic and fast! I'm sure it must have been bittersweet for Herb to see his frail father sitting in the front seat admiring this toy like a kid in a candy store. We wanted to believe the best. We wanted hope that he could fight this battle and win. But it didn't take more than ten weeks to see a patriarch become feeble and weak.

One morning, as I was heading off to work, Dad asked me if he could have a minute. He gifted me with a 14-carat gold crucifix ring. He told me that even though other family members wanted it, he wanted me to have it. He asked me to promise that I would keep Catholicism as a religion for our future children one day, and I agreed with tears in my eyes and a lump in my throat. That honestly was one of the most special gifts I've ever received. It meant so much to me that he wanted me to have it. I still wear this ring on my right index finger today, decades later. I felt sad because I knew he would never get to be a part of our wedding day.

It was Veterans Day as Herb and I were driving to Shepherd Hill for a football game. I strongly felt it important to ask him if he gave his father a kiss goodbye. He said no, so we turned around and went back to the house. Herb intentionally gave his dad a big hug and kiss. When we came home after the game, we learned his dad had passed away. Herb was devastated, as were the rest of us. But I was so thankful Herb had that last meaningful moment with his dad.

Herb was very close to his dad, and he turned to work to dull the pain. The busier he was, the better. What better way to keep distracted than to delve into work and find value in earning money. He confided in me and expressed how, since the death of his father, there had been an emptiness, a hole deep in his heart that ached. We were all shattered. It didn't make sense. Where was God? Was there a God? If so, why did He let this happen? It wasn't fair. It was such an evil disease—relentless, torturous, and merciless. There are just some things a person should never have to go through. With little privacy in a house full of ten and one bathroom off the kitchen, often you would hear him getting sick. At times there was nothing more you could do than hold the bucket for him and try to hold back the reflex of vomiting yourself. There's nothing worse than watching someone you love suffering. *Cancer* was a *C*-letter word we didn't even like to repeat. It felt like a horrible nightmare. How can someone who was so significant be gone? He was the authoritative figure over the home, and now we all felt vulnerable. The atmosphere changed. I tried not to grieve in front of the others. I felt like I only knew him for a short amount of time.

Herb's mom was strong for months. She cared for him when he was ill and would try to keep "normalcy" for the sake of all the kids. She rarely complained and had no one to confide in either. She was pregnant at the age of sixteen and seventeen when she married the man. March of that same year, they celebrated their twentieth wedding anniversary. But let's face it, all hell broke loose. There was no comfort or consolation. By this time, dysfunction was rampant, and there was no order. During the grief process, Herb's mom would either drink or gamble to pass the time. I remember desperately trying to wake her up so she could care for the children. I felt obligated to take on a more responsible role and was the one helping the children get ready for school and on the bus. I would prepare meals and try to keep the house in order, but it was no use. I had no control, and it was too overwhelming.

We were celebrating Herb's brother Keith's graduation. I was nineteen. We had many family and friends over the house. More or less, I was considered a goody two-shoes and took great pride in the fact that I never smoked a cigarette, drank alcohol, or did any drugs.

There was a feeling of anxiety mixed with awkwardness. I don't remember who bought the keg, but I gave in and decided I was going to try beer for the first time. I really wasn't impressed with the taste but finished my cup anyway. I found myself feeling lighter, caring less, and giggly. So I had another. Officially, that was the first time I experienced a buzz and became quite intoxicated. Even though I exhibited foolish behavior, it felt freeing not to care. I even boasted that I didn't suffer from a hangover the next day.

One day when Herb came home, he surprised me with a new business adventure. He wasn't the predictable type. He told me as he was driving through Worcester, he noticed a breakfast diner was for sale. He made the decision to dump his plumbing job and try something new. I was taken back but thrilled because we all needed something different. When he drove me there (to peek), I noticed it was just a three-story apartment building with a small restaurant located on the first floor. We weren't buying the building, just the business. His mom loaned us the money to start up, and we began our new and exciting endeavor of Herbie's Diner. We hired a young artist we knew to hand-paint murals of our family as cartoon characters. One painting was of Herb standing by his '68 Chevelle. It was light beige with black racing stripes. The guy did such a great job and depicted every detail. Another one was of me with my long brown curly hair and a tight white dress; I pretty much looked like Dolly Parton from the neck down, thanks to his animation. And my favorite is one of the whole family packed like sardines in a car that looked just like the Beverly Hillbillies! It was comic relief. This was the first time we were finding joy again since Herb's father's death. We hung up old posters of Marilyn Monroe, the Three Stooges, and Groucho Marx.

I have fond memories of our diner. I will always remember the first day we opened. It was absolutely hilarious! An older man came in and sat down at one of the tables patiently waiting for a waitress to take his order. All I can say is both Herb's mom, Denise, and I froze. I suggested she take his order. She refused and told me to do it. We went back and forth for a couple minutes; all the while Herb was growing extremely impatient with the both of us. You see, I had no experience ever as a waitress, and neither did Denise. In fact, Herb was never a cook either! What in the world were we doing? We were so useless because we were hiding under the counter by the cash register in tears from laughing so hard. As you probably guessed by now, it was Herb who took the customer's order. Good stuff. We were fortunate to know of a friend nicknamed "Beef" that had a natural talent for cooking. He shared a secret recipe for the best fish and chips and taught us some basics to becoming a short-order cook.

It wasn't uncommon for the entire football team to come for spaghetti and meatballs. Family from both sides and friends would drop in to visit and enjoy a home-cooked meal. It really was a pleasurable time.

Promises Unkept

But God showed his great love for us by sending
Christ to die for us while we were still sinners.

—Romans 5:8 NLT

Why a father would burden his oldest son at the young age of twenty on his deathbed is beyond me. Herb promised his dad that he would take care of his mom and his brothers. It wasn't a reasonable or realistic request, if you ask me.

Rebellion was rearing its ugly head by this point. We were putting in over sixty hours a week at the diner, and Herb was working full-time for an oil-burner company out of Spencer because we needed to supplement our income. When people came to the diner, they would often ask where Herb was. It was Herb they wanted to see behind the grill cooking their food; after all, the name of the restaurant was *Herbie's* Diner!

We were drinking heavily on weekends and partying a lot. Herb would go off with the guys to gentlemen's clubs (that term is such an oxymoron), and I was hanging out with my girlfriends flaunting my figure in skimpy clothes for all the wrong attention. Denise was still youthful. She passed off easily as my sister, and we would sometimes dress as twins. Our standard for morals were usually compared with the people we hung out with. You could manipulate a man for a drink at the bar and even dance seductively if you didn't cheat (sexually). We learned the skill of country-music line dancing. Some of the most popular dances were the "Boot Scootin' Boogie," the "Watermelon Crawl," and (my favorite at the time) "Trashy Women" (I couldn't dance to that song and keep a straight face).

"Functionally dysfunctional" would best describe this time. We had a futon in the back room of the kitchen at the diner and would take turns passing out from exhaustion. We built rapport with the regulars. Some of our close customers would open for us. They would knock on the glass door to wake us up and put their own pot of coffee on. There were a few guys who were attracted to my mother-in-law, and I felt like a mother hen watching out for her.

My uncle Mark was going through a difficult divorce at the time. He lost a lot of weight and would come by for a meal regularly. He worked for an oil company with Herb's brother Keith. You could tell my Uncle Mark had other motives for coming by the restaurant. It wasn't until years later that Denise confessed that she and my uncle would rendezvous for coffee. I must believe that not only did Keith have some influence on the decision for them to hook up, but maybe Herbie's Diner was an impact as well. As for Herb and me, we were beginning to plan our wedding.

By this point, we were hardly getting much sleep. We had to be up by five in the morning to get to Worcester to open the breakfast diner. Herb's brothers weren't respecting the home. There was no father figure anymore. Rules went out the window. Herb and I did try to gain order. Our roles changed from kids to not wannabe parents. Keith and Sean, Herb's two younger brothers, would throw parties at the house and sneak alcohol. It was Sean's graduation, and both of Herb's brothers invited the entire senior class. They literally had well over a hundred kids swarming at the house. There were several kegs and pitched tents in the back of the field. My efforts to at least minimize the potential for an accident was to collect keys so they could not drive home drunk. I had a large punch bowl filled with keys. We would refer to that event as a "mini" Woodstock.

The neighbors, no doubt, put a complaint with the police. They came and tried to shut it all down. They even chased some of the kids through the woods with flashlights. Even though Denise did not condone this, the repercussions could have been serious for her. I believe God had His hand of protection on her, on all of us, frankly. As an adult, I look back and think how tolerant the neighbors were of us. We weren't a quiet household. Many times the boys would burn rubber up and down our road. There was no denying who did it: the long black strips were always left by the driveway of our home like a trophy of some sort being showcased.

I was at my breaking point. As difficult as it was for me to make Herb choose, I told him it was going to have to be me or his family. I couldn't live like this anymore. Stress was severe, and I didn't see a way we could fix it. During an argument, he told me to get my boots on because we were going for a ride. Even though we were only about twenty minutes away, it felt like we took a trip to Vermont.

He took me to Brookfield. I had no idea what we were doing. We stopped and got out of the truck, trudging through knee-high snow in darkness. He kept his headlights on and presented a hideous aqua-blue mobile home set on a wooded lot. He expressed to me that he was negotiating a deal with the seller and that this would be the very first home of our own together. I was fearful and overjoyed all at once. I cried and told him that I would make it a beautiful home. I was so thankful for our humble beginnings. Even though it wasn't what I always envisioned, I was desperate. This place had five acres of land. It was right off Route 148. Finally, we could have privacy and peace. The land was loaded with ledge. It was doubtful that it was a buildable lot, but we had faith that maybe someday we would try. The seller was gracious to sell it to us being as young as we were with limited funds. He agreed to hold part of the mortgage for us, and we would pay him a monthly payment.

It was a painful decision to come up with the deposit for our new home. Herb had no other financial means other than to sell the Mustang. I know Herb struggled with feelings of guilt when we moved, but I was grateful for his sacrifice.

We served fish and chips every Friday at the diner, and it was right before the rush when we noticed the deep fryer was not cooking the oil properly. I assumed the oil needed to be changed, so I drove down to the store to replace the oil in time for lunch. When I returned, I came to a sight I was not anticipating. The firetrucks were there. My first thought was the upstairs tenants. I hoped that everyone was safe and able to evacuate. It was determined that the fryolator was malfunctioning. The oil was boiling in the fryolator, but the knobs were broken, giving a false reading of the actual temperature.

Thank God, no one was hurt and the damage was isolated. The fire chief mandated that if we were to continue business, we needed to update the system in the building with expensive sprinklers. We did not have tens of thousands of dollars to invest into a building we didn't own, so we cut our losses and moved on.

I wish I could say that was the last time I had a run-in with fire, but about a month before our wedding, I had the bright idea that I was going to handcraft my own centerpieces and create floating candles for the reception hall. I bought all the supplies and was eager to begin. I never made them before. How difficult could it be? I began to melt the wax on the cooktop stove in the kitchen of the old house. The wax liquefied and caught fire, and the flames were dancing on the ceiling. My biggest concern was that the children were asleep in their beds upstairs. I was nervous the fire would catch on the old wooden beams that were exposed. I panicked and grabbed the handle to the saucepan and headed to the kitchen door. As soon as I pulled the door open, I heard a noise I had never heard before. I heard the powerful breath of fire. When I opened the door, it gave the fire more oxygen and caused a back draft. The flames lightly scorched my upper body, arms, and shoulders. It also fried the hair on my forehead, eyebrows, nostrils, and eyelashes. There was a distinct odor of singed hair.

I threw the pan full of flames outside and screamed. Herb ran from the garage and met me at the door. I was at a loss for words. He asked me if the fire was inside. I told him I thought the house was clear. He glanced at me and tried to reassure me by saying, "You don't look that bad. Just don't look in the mirror." What did that mean exactly? That bad? I knew I was burned, but I didn't know to what degree. All I could think about was how this would affect my appearance on our wedding day. I quickly ran to the bathroom to check my reflection while Herb drew me a cool tub. He brought me to the hospital. I had superficial second-degree burns on my arms that eventually changed the pigmentation of my skin and made me look tan year-round. I know the situation could have turned out a lot worse. I was beyond grateful the house didn't go up in flames and that the children were spared.

I'm pretty sure it would be lottery odds for a bride to wake up with pink eye the day of her wedding—lucky me! We wanted the actual wedding day to be on June 3 because that would have been exactly five years as a couple, but leap year interrupted our plans. So we decided to have the wedding on June 1, two days before our official five-year anniversary. We knew it would confuse us. As a precaution, we made sure to have the wedding date engraved on the inside of our matching wedding bands. I will admit, I've had to rely on that measure more than once.

I was three months shy of being twenty-one. I looked like a princess. My wedding gown was all I hoped it would be. Denise was thoughtful to buy my dress for me. It reminded me of Glenda the good witch in *The Wizard of Oz*. I had remarkably large puffy sleeves, a size 3 waist, and a large hooplike bell-shaped skirt that touched the floor. There were shimmering sequins on the bodice and tulle everywhere! I had elegant embroidered sleeves with a point at the wrist line and a high-collared neck that reminded me of the Victorian era. There must have been fifty covered buttons on the back. My train was long but easily adjustable to button up behind me for dancing. I had a professional manicure with acrylic nails (they were much too exaggerated and long). It took quite a long time for my cousin Amy and Katie to curl my hair with the curling irons. My veil had white nylon roses that crowned my head with more tulle trailing behind me. On my left leg, I put a light-blue garter along with a white thong that Herb would later reveal as a prank during our reception. I repurposed my white prom shoes to save some money. I was always into the details. Everything had to be perfect. I concealed every blemish.

I was very upset that I had pink eye. The doctors weren't open on Saturdays, so Amy shared some eye ointment she had in her medicine cabinet with me. I was concerned the photographs would forever mark the infection in my eyes. I didn't want people to assume I was high (not that I ever was). I should have known better. Was the pink eye a punishment? Herb forbade me to go to the tanning salon, but I wanted to have the perfect sun-kissed shade on my skin.

He wasn't going to know anyway, so I went. And don't you think I'd know better than to share goggles? Not me! I believe I got pink eye from someone who must have had it and used the community goggles! I eventually confessed this to Herb, and I got the usual sarcastic response of, "I told you so!"

These were the days before GPS and MapQuest. I always made a better passenger than a driver. I was terrible at giving or receiving directions. A friend of a family member offered to get us a limo. But when he pulled up, I was less than impressed. And what made matters worse was he had no idea where the church was, and neither did I! All I knew was to find Temple Street in Worcester at St. John's Church.

I may have thought it was a bit humorous that I was approximately forty-five minutes late to my own wedding. I'm not so proud as I've matured over the years. It is very narcissistic and inconsiderate to consistently be late, but how much worse is it the day of your wedding?

The priest almost convinced Herb that I wasn't coming, and he was going to treat Herb to a beer. We even managed to frustrate the caterers, which happened to be parents of a good friend of Herb's from high school. How much pressure do you think the caterers were under when you must keep a buffet for two hundred and fifty people warm? My twin sister, Keri, was my maid of honor. The total amount of people in our wedding party was eighteen, including ourselves. There were two adorable flower girls, one of whom I can't wait to share with you later about (my younger cousin Erika). We chose Herb's godson little Larry—who, by the way, was so cute—as our ring bearer. I think his two front teeth were missing; he was probably about six years of age. I sewed the lacy heart-shaped pillow with two white ribbons that secured our golden wedding bands.

I requested that my sister sing a song at the ceremony. One of the sad consequences of being late was she was unable to gift us our song. She even went out of the way to invite two of her friends from her college to join her. I really felt sorry about that. If I could go back and change a few things, that would be one of them. I lent Keri a piece of costume jewelry that belonged to our Nana (our great-grandmother). It appeared to be blue topaz and tanzanite gemstones with silver settings. One of my favorite flowers was the blue rose. They were very special to me. They were rare and known specifically as an angel rose. Did you know that blue roses signify true love? True blue roses do not exist in nature. My Memere was known for having a green thumb and was well versed in a wide variety of flowers and plants. When I was little, I would play in her yard and admire the varieties of perennials in her garden. Some of my favorite fragrances were of the purple lilacs near her birdfeeder in the back of her home. All my bridesmaids looked stunning in their blue-rose vintage-print gowns. As they walked down the aisle, they stood under their white laced parasols.

The party favors were homemade. I saved most of the roses over the years that Herb would buy for me. I decided to make pot-pourri sachets adorned with faux blue roses. The cake topper was most fitting. It was a bride pulling the tuxedo tails of the groom as he appeared to be escaping from her clutches.

Herb looked quite attractive in his formal tuxedo. He had a white bow tie, matching cummerbund, and a crisp starchy white dress shirt accessorized with cuff links. His shoes were shiny, and he had coordinating tails on his jacket to match the cake topper. I was so used to him in a T-shirt, jeans, and work boots. He's not a vain high-maintenance man. He's naturally masculine and makes no effort to impress anyone. That's what I love about him.

As I walked down the center aisle of the church, I was honored to have my brother, Nathan, and my mom give me away. I don't know who comes up with these wedding traditions, but it was time to cut the cake. Another talented family member agreed to make me my dream cake. It was gorgeous. A blue fountain that really worked was on the first tier. There were six multi-sized cakes with glass ladders, white and blue icing, and yes, blue roses galore! As the DJ was giving instructions for me to feed my groom, I knew it was now or never. So I smushed his piece right up his nostrils. It was his turn to feed me. I braced myself as Herb grabbed an entire cake (the one you're supposed to save for the first-year anniversary). I begged him not to destroy that particular one; he obliged. He had no mercy: he not only had his new bride in a headlock, but he slammed a giant cake right in my face and broke three fake nails while doing it! It was true love.

"Close your eyes and point." That's what Herb said as we held a map of New England on our lap. My finger landed on Bar Harbor, Maine. And that's where we drove for our honeymoon. We had close to six hundred bucks left from the wedding. I can remember wanting to take a tour to go whale watching. We entertained the thought of taking the ferry over to Nova Scotia, but we just couldn't afford it. We had the expenses of our trailer, utilities, two auto payments, and debt from the diner. But we still found inexpensive ways to enjoy our time together.

Searching for answers

So why are you trying to find out the future by consulting mediums and psychics? Do not listen to their whisperings and mutterings. Can the living find out the future from the dead? Why not ask your God?

—Isaiah 8:19 NLT

Sometimes in life, when most things just don't seem to make sense anymore, you start to have a curiosity from all those unanswered questions. You need reasoning. Answers would be helpful, and we didn't have direction. We were lost. Where should we go from here?

One beautiful sunny day, we were at Hampton Beach with Herb's family. We took a walk on the boardwalk in search for the bathrooms and was enticed by this small colorful tent. There was a sign on the front among many that gave their fair price for a palm reading. Another one advertised tarot cards. I was a fan at the time of reading my horoscope regularly but never actually accepted a session with someone who claimed to know my future. I was interested but very hesitant and somewhat skeptical. The temptation was hard to resist. We thought it was harmless. We were introduced to a woman by the name of Madam Jean. She looked the part: she had on the long fancy garb and the dramatic eye makeup. It was quite entertaining to be invited into her canopy. She seemed quite nice and offered to tell us our future with her crystal ball.

She got my attention when she started to say a few things that a perfect stranger should have no knowledge of. She warned Herb that he was to remain away from motorcycles because she sensed the presence of the devil. I was blown away and intrigued. I had goose bumps. The hair on my arms were lifted like static electricity.

What did she just say? How in the world could she have known that recently Herb just sold his teal-green Suzuki Katana motorcycle with the mileage of 666? She went on to warn him that he potentially could lose his legs if he rode a motorcycle. We certainly didn't want that to happen! This wasn't exactly great news. We were looking for hope, not impending doom!

Lastly, she went on to tell us we would have septic issues with our home. *Yeah, right! Who is this lady? She has no idea what she's talking about. This is all just a bunch of made-up garbage.* I handed her money and walked out of her tent even more confused, and paranoid.

When I was running to the arms of my true love in my teens, so was my sister, Keri. Her true love was Jesus. She became obsessed with the Catholic religion. We were brought up Protestant, whatever that meant. We believed in God, yes, but knew very little about religion. It was rare we would go to church. Maybe on a holiday, or if my great-aunt Mona and her husband, Paul, would bring us to the First Assembly of God. Keri was drawn to St. Joseph's Church on the corner of Route 20 in Charlton, where our bus stop was. I always thought Keri was odd, but that was her thing. Right out of high school, she joined a convent in Still River, Massachusetts.

She used to jokingly call me a heathen. Again, I knew she was teasing me, but I still had no clue what a heathen was. Was a heathen destined for hell? A sinner that had no hope? She would give gifts in the mail of beautiful colored glass rosary beads with little cards that gave instructions of how to recite a prayer to Mary, the mother of Jesus. It was all so confusing and, honestly, strange. I never really felt comfortable going into a large cathedral/church. It was dark, cold, and full of haughty, religious people, in my opinion. Yes, I was a critical person then. I barely knew the Our Father prayer. And when the congregation would make the sign of the cross by touching their foreheads and motioning below the chest and over their shoulders from left to right, I just thought that was bizarre as well. And what in the world did you genuflect for? I also struggled greatly with the whole confession thing. Why would anyone go to another human being, a priest, to confess their sins? It was my understanding that God should be the only one to forgive a person's sins. You'd never catch me confessing my sins to a man, that's for sure; I don't care what kind of collar he wore.

There were times I would drive out to visit her at the convent. The nuns seemed to adore her. They were kind to me as well. I even remember taking on a short sewing job once to make some extra money. Keri tried to share her faith with me often. I wanted nothing to do with it. She could keep her Jesus. I was doing just fine, thank you very much. I was glad Keri found happiness, but a part of me wished she didn't live in such strict conditions. There were a lot of rules that I didn't understand. I would have to dress modestly when I went to visit and wear these lacy doilies over my head. I felt so prissy and foolish. But I would do just about anything for the chance to be with my twin.

I remember the time Keri came to visit Memere's house with her superior, Sister Mary Michelle, and we were sitting outside at the picnic table. Keri was determined to save my soul. She threw holy water on my head. Sister Mary Michelle corrected her efforts. Her attempt to save me was in vain because it was not of my own free will. I was the one who needed to decide. It wasn't up to Keri to "save" me.

Let me be clear—no, I did not marry my cousin! Herb and I got married *first*. Herb's mom, Denise, married my uncle Mark (my mother's brother) less than a year after our wedding. I'm not going to lie and say it was easy. At first, a part of us thought, shouldn't she wait a little longer before getting in a serious relationship? But where's the rule book for this stuff? We felt torn at first because we wanted to be loyal to Dad. But the bottom line was, he was gone, and they seemed to really be happy with each other. They both went through some very challenging times. It was refreshing to see them find companionship again. My uncle was a little younger than Denise, by four years. I was the matron of honor, and Herb was chosen as the best man. It was a small gathering. They were married by the justice of the peace in an intimate ceremony at the Sagendorph mansion in Spencer. It was built in 1876 and is located on High Street. A beautiful wrap-around porch with a gazebo accents the front of the house with double doors leading to the grand foyer. I attempted to go blonde for this occasion and failed miserably. My hair turned pumpkin orange. My uncle

Mark was a funny guy. He was a dependable hard worker. He was a father of two boys from his first marriage. He had old-fashioned principles and was stubborn as an ox at times. He loved old country music, especially George Jones, and enjoyed car shows. He laughed a lot and had a sarcastic sense of humor (it was usually at the expense of someone else). He wasn't the most affectionate person; I think we only hugged on Christmas. But one thing we knew was, his love for Herb's mom was sincere. And she not only loved him as a husband but also as a close friend.

Holidays were less chaotic. We only had one place to go instead of trying to squeeze in time with both sides of the family, which was appreciated. We used to drive to Worcester to spend time with the Seymour side of the family, then go back to Spencer to my side. When Dad died, it wasn't long before Grampa and Grandma Seymour passed on as well. That side of the family was falling apart, and it was sad that holiday celebrations weren't the same anymore.

I was just hired full-time as a teller at a small-town local bank. The bank was inside a grocery store. I adjusted my shabby style of attire to something more appropriate, being in a professional setting. Holly, whom I thought at first to be snobbish, was an assistant manager there. It wasn't long before we became friends. She had light-brown natural curly hair. She was pregnant with her first child. I felt bad for her because she had carpal tunnel syndrome and had to wear a black brace on her hand when she counted money. What a colorful group of people with many different personalities. If you've been to this bank, you would easily know whom I'm referring to when I say we had a very flamboyant man, a heavyset woman with a Brazilian accent, and a petite redhead who drank too much coffee. There was a young kid named Ray whom I assumed was Asian. His sidekick's name was Tim. And there was an animal lover named Cheyanne who blushed easily. My boss's name was Matt. He wasn't very intimidating at all. He was young and passive. The crew who worked there was a lot of fun. I felt like I fit in just like a piece to a jigsaw puzzle. I learned the customers and all the policies and procedures that are necessary for working in a financial institution. It didn't take long to develop relationships that would seem more like family than just friends.

They say when you go through something traumatic, it is possible to have memory loss. There definitely were a couple years we were dazed. We were still caring for Mom and Dad's old house. I was so erratic with emotion. Herb remembers that I ran out to greet him one day when he came home from work. I was beyond thrilled with a pregnancy test proving he was going to be a daddy! I was not a private person and hastily called everyone to share the enthusiastic news. I've heard some women wait cautiously at least till the second trimester before they tell others. I was an optimist and a terrible keeper of secrets! We painted the old brown house and brightened it up with a sunny shade of yellow. We put a coat of baby-blue exterior paint on the shutters. We gave the neglected home a lot of love and tried to fix it up for minimal cost.

I was in my twenties. A part of me was selfish and immature. I was a binge drinker almost every weekend; most of our friends still had freedom. I cared about superficial things like my appearance and my social life. Then I had thoughts that all my dreams would have to come to an end because I was going to be a mom. Ever since I was a little girl, I always wanted to be a singer. A country music artist. I loved the Judds, Reba McEntire, Loretta Lynn, Patsy Cline and Dolly. Even though I didn't pursue this dream, I figured I could kiss it goodbye. Being a momma wasn't glamorous. It was hard work and, as far as I was concerned, martyrdom.

I had mixed emotions and doubts, which made me feel guilty. People seemed genuinely happy for us. Maybe I was ready to be a mommy. Maybe what I was experiencing was completely normal. But who would I confide in? These aren't thoughts a woman can share. I didn't want to seem unstable or, worse, ungrateful for this beautiful gift! I never gave abortion a thought. I just struggled with the permanence of parenthood. It sounded like an eighteen-year prison sentence.

When I went to the doctors for an ultrasound, I wanted so badly for the technician to send me home with a black-and-white picture of our little baby, who was about the size of a grain of rice. I was able to see the heartbeat. It was incredibly fast, like the flickering of a firefly. The technician sent me off without a picture to go home with. I was disappointed and suspicious.

It was January the year 2000. Another leap year. We survived Y2K. My grandfather in Vermont lost the battle to cancer. I drove up with some of my family to pay my respects. Herb was not able to go. I was nearing the end of my first trimester. I was resting at my great-uncle Bruce's home. I was reclined in a chair and was very concerned because I felt cramping and pain. When I went to the bathroom, I noticed right away that I was bleeding. I wasn't prepared emotionally or physically for what was about to happen. I was thankful that my cousin Amy drove me a few hours back home to Massachusetts on such short notice. I suppressed many of the details that follow.

I was devastated. I blamed myself. Was I eating enough? Resting enough? Did I remember to take my prenatal vitamins? Could it be from the stress of going to Vermont? The funeral? Maybe I was being punished for my selfishness and doubts. I felt like I failed my husband. The worst part was facing everyone and telling them there will be no baby. I regretted telling everyone in the first place. I should have just kept my mouth shut. I do remember locking myself in the upstairs bathroom sitting in a tub of blood crying and feeling ashamed—feeling like a loser, defeated, heartbroken; looking at the remains of this tiny undeveloped baby in the palm of my hand, wondering what went wrong. Another sad fact was, I didn't know how to include my husband in my state of grief. He was mourning too. Unintentionally, we silently pushed away from each other.

We knew we wanted to try again soon. Human nature fights for what it can't have. We refused to give up. Fewer than 5 percent of women will have two miscarriages in a row; with those odds, we had hope. We both were young and healthy. Maybe the last miscarriage was just a fluke. It was only a matter of months, and we were happy to announce we were pregnant again!

I didn't want to be superstitious. I couldn't contain the joy. Herb was so much more reserved than I was. I believed it was safe to share the wonderful news again with friends and family. We were so happy. This time, we were going to have a baby. I took extra care of myself, and Herb helped me when he could. All the right changes were happening to my body. I was nauseous, my chest was tender, and I had food cravings. I required cat naps during my lunch break in the back room at work. All my coworkers were very supportive too. All was well; I had no signs of spotting.

I approached the end of my first trimester. It was déjà vu. Can you believe we relived the same nightmare twice? I went to the emergency room in Worcester. This time, I brought the fetus in a Ziploc bag for testing. I wanted answers. We didn't bounce back this time, though. We suffered terribly. We felt so duped. I cried a lot. This just wasn't fair. Why does this keep happening to us? Again, where is God in all of this? And don't tell me everything happens for a reason—I was done with that!

I had a tremendous amount of difficulty coping by this point. I went to my doctor and told him I was suffering from anxiety and depression. He recommended I begin Wellbutrin to alleviate my symptoms. I wasn't typically the kind of person that depended on prescriptions unless it was the necessary dosage of antibiotics for an infection or ibuprofen for pain. I went on the medication for a few months. It did seem to take the edge off. I was at least able to function, even if I was in a zombie state. I was numb. I was there, just not present. Herb told me he wanted me to take myself off the prescription. He was concerned for me. So I did. I couldn't see the person I was, but he could. I was withdrawn and way too quiet.

The drinking got worse. I just wanted to have a good time and forget my sorrows. I didn't consider myself an alcoholic. I wouldn't label myself as one. I had my own preconceptions of what an alcoholic was. I was different. I could hold down a job. I was faithful to my husband. I was fine. And besides, I could stop at any time if I wanted to.

Do I Have Your Attention?

God speaks again and again though people do not recognize it. He speaks in dreams in visions of the night. When sleep falls on people as they lie in their bed. He whispers in their ear and terrifies them with this warning.

—Job 33:14–16 NLT

We went on vacation with a large group of family to Lake Champlain in Vermont. We went to a family campground in the mountains and pitched tents. We have relatives that live in Vermont who joined us as well. It was always nice when we'd get together to catch up and reminisce. What I will tell you is probably the most frightening experience I've ever gone through. I've been through some difficult stuff, but nothing has ever compared to this night. The day was good. We casually sat at the picnic table with family and enjoyed good conversation and food together. Nothing was unusual about the day. It was time to retire and get some sleep. This is what I recall in vivid detail.

I was in a tall building. It was a high-riser in a large city. There were windows all around me. I was alone. I could clearly see outside to the other tall buildings and the view of the sky. The sky was turning shades of red and deep purple with eerie clouds of gray. I was struck with terror. I was paralyzed with fear. I had a notion the buildings were going to collapse. It was an apocalyptic event. I knew my time was about to end. I was powerless. And I began to have a conversation with God Almighty.

I wasn't ready to die yet. But my greatest concern was not for myself, which made no sense to me at the time. I asked God, What about Herb? What about my mother? What was going to happen to them? I didn't seem to have concern for my sister. I didn't hear an audible voice, but I was still very scared. He was speaking to my spirit, and I knew exactly where the conversation was leading to. I had an assignment, if you will. Even though He didn't appear to me visually, I knew His presence was undoubtedly there with me. I said to the Lord, *Why me? Why not Keri? She's the nun, not me.* I felt that I wasn't capable or qualified to help them. He insisted that I was to be the one who needed to tell them about Him. But how? All I know was, I didn't want them to perish, and we were running out of time to save them. Then all the buildings around me began to crumble and fall. All I could see were clouds of debris. The loudest, bloodcurdling scream came from my mouth; and when I woke, I disturbed the campground. I was trembling and frantically crying. I couldn't stop. My aunt comforted me, and I shared the nightmare I had with the ones who stayed awake. I refused to go back to sleep. I did not want to enter that dream ever again. To be honest, I didn't have a full understanding of the meaning of this dream until subsequent years. I will explain the revelation that came to me about this dream later.

Herb found out from his boss at work that Mom and Dad's house was in the newspaper because the real estate taxes were not being paid. The threat of losing that property for unpaid taxes was upsetting. How could this be neglected? Herb was frustrated and concerned. We always dreamed that someday we were going to build our dream house on that land in the back, just like we envisioned years earlier. Before Dad passed away, he verbally told Herb that, as a wedding gift, we could have one acre of land to build on. There was no last will. We moved back to the house in hopes to protect it from being taken away, and we rented our mobile home to a distant family member. It was unfortunate, but Herb began selling some of Dad's assets to pay the taxes that were in the rears. Herb's brothers didn't understand what was going on and would sometimes accuse Herb of taking the cash from the items that were sold.

There was a great moment of testing for us. It was so subtle and could have passed off as a gift in disguise. Herb's mom, Denise, offered to give me and Herb the house. Free and clear. Wow, what an opportunity. But something just didn't feel right about it. I believe Mom had good intentions. She just wanted us to take it off her hands and be rid of the responsibility. Perhaps bless us. I strongly feel God intervened and gave us wisdom to not accept the offer even though we wanted to. When I gave it great thought, I told Herb we could never do that. Looking ahead further down the road, if we were given the home, his brothers most likely would never receive their share of their inheritance because we would have had to put a mortgage on the property to pay back taxes. Most likely, the land would be locked. We did not want to be selfish or deceive his brothers for our own personal gain, so we politely declined Denise's offer.

We were both working full-time. I don't think I even hit the nine-dollar-an-hour mark. We saved up enough money to perc the land adjacent to the house. There were three buildable lots and the old house. We were motivated to build our dream home and were so happy when the perc test came in as an approved buildable lot. We compromised and accepted that the house wouldn't be on the exact spot we thought of earlier because the cost would have been too expensive to put in a road to reach the back.

We never saw it coming, but Denise was offered money from a local contractor—mind you, the same one we hired—to purchase the very land we were planning to build on. There was confusion, disappointment, and yes, we even felt betrayed. That lot was sold, and so was the one beside it. Now there was only one buildable lot and the old house left. Not the best scenario for three sons. We were out of the money we invested. There was no communication at that time. Just a lot of confusion.

Several months passed by. We didn't want to fight over land, and we didn't want to feud with family. It was hard, but not impossible to forgive. The fact was the house and land belonged to Denise. Period. We gave up the dream of building there and decided we were going to attempt to build on our own five acres of land with the mobile home. To our surprise, even though there was a tremendous amount of ledge, it was, in fact, a buildable lot! So we began to design blueprints for a Cape and knocked down that hideous aluminum caboose (a.k.a. the mobile home).

Finally, we were going to have a beautiful home of our own. We had a lot of support from family and friends. Coming from a trade school, we had a lot of connections to people who had knowledge on how to build, how to install electrical, and how to plumb. Our friend Craigy spent many hours wiring our home. His dad pitched in too. We felt very blessed and thankful. We would cover the cost of material. When we compensated our workers, they were generous and didn't charge us the full rate. Some of our friends would barter the labor for future plumbing favors. Craigy built a house up the road from us; my honey was able to return the favor and helped him plumb his new house. We had helpful friends who would do just about anything for us, and vice versa.

You may ask, why is it so important to you to have a nice home? I'm sure we must sound materialistic and shallow. It was more about accomplishment, about attaining a goal we set for ourselves. We wanted to have a better life than how we came up. It was something we had to prove to ourselves. We refused to be defined by the world according to our childhood beginnings.

I moved a lot when I was young. More times than I can remember. I must have been about nine or so when my mother wanted to move us from the city of Worcester to a small town. She found a place in Charlton. Our residence was at the top of Carpenter Hill Road. The view was breathtaking. We were surrounded by cornfields and open pastures. The aroma gave proof to the dairy cows nearby. There were also wild raspberries and rhubarb. We enjoyed the mature apple tree in the front yard. We had a huge pine tree that peaked high. You probably could see Route 20 from the top. I'm just kidding! Route 20 was about a mile down the street. I've climbed that tree to the top with my brother. We were so proud of ourselves. We yelled down to Mom, "Hey, Mom, look at us!" She looked as small as the size of an ant. That should give you a rough idea of how high we were. The tip of that tree was thin, and Nate was balancing on one side while I was bearing weight on the other. We were swaying back and forth. Mom scolded us and demanded we get down immediately. We knew what was coming; we had the pace of a sloth inching our way down the branches of that pine.

Even though we were out in the country, the house was in much need of renovation and repair. I was told it was an old chicken coop years earlier. There were exposed studs throughout the house—old electrical wiring, no sheetrock, Pink Panther insulation stuffed into the barren walls, and we had minimal space. It was a fixer-upper. And that's great if you can afford to fix it up, but we couldn't right away. It took many years for improvements. I wish I wasn't embarrassed, but I was. We didn't have a working bathroom. We used a porta potty for our toilet for three years. You know, the ones you'd use for camping? With every pull of the lever, you'd see dark-blue water that flushed all the matter into a small holding tank that my mom's boyfriend had the honor of emptying on a weekly basis. We also sponge-bathed in the sink and would take a trip to Memere's every Sunday to take a bath.

I know my mom tried to do her best. There was a lack of support. She didn't have a lot of opportunities that are available nowadays. She was a survivor herself. I'm sure it was painfully difficult for her. Neither was my biological father nor Nathan's paying child support. She didn't marry and was labeled a single mother of three kids on welfare. It wasn't easy for any of us. Let me help you understand why it was so important to Herb and me to break free from poverty.

Have you ever had to chase after your school bus? My siblings and I did. Why? Mrs. Merina, a mother to one of the popular boys in my grade, was our bus driver. She appeared to have it all. She was put together, had short black hair, wore makeup, had nice clothes, nice house—you know, she seemed to live a normal life. What other explanation was there that she would purposely drive by us three kids as we were waiting by the side of the road near our house? She sometimes would put the brakes on and stop at least a hundred feet past where we were. We would try to catch up to her. Many times, she would just drive on by. It's hard not to take that stuff personal. You think an adult would know better than to pick on kids. I will never forget the time she stopped the bus on the side of the road and instructed everyone to check their shoes. It was obvious by the odor that someone stepped in dog crap. I reluctantly admitted it was me. I was horrified. I had to get off the bus and wipe my feet in the grass before I was allowed back in. These moments can mortify a child. It was bad enough we had to run after our bus like a dog, but how much worse is it when you're singled out in front of the whole bus? She even accused my sister of stealing her daughter's Trapper Keeper once. Keri did take it, maybe she thought she could have it for herself because it was left on the seat. Finders keepers, Trapper Keepers?

Our mom bumped into Mrs. Merina unexpectedly one day. She was working as a bartender. My mom made a scene and defended us publicly and warned that bus driver she better not ever pass by us again. That was a highlighted memory I will always cherish. It felt good to be avenged.

Even though we were kids, you still know when others are looking down on you. We were the kids who wore hand-me-downs from our older cousins. We didn't go to the salon or barber for haircuts; we were victims to my aunt Karen's scissors. Even though she meant well, my bangs were usually crooked. And when other kids got to go to school with the latest toys and gadgets, we were jealous and felt sorry for ourselves. We could never afford family vacations to Disney or rent a beach house for a week like my aunt Donna could.

You know those cardboard boxes filled during Thanksgiving with a turkey, some canned items, and boxed food? We would find it dropped off at our doorstep. We were on the receiving end of donations during Christmastime too. Yes, it was kind of our community to reach out and acknowledge our family was in need. There were times I was appreciative. Maybe all of this doesn't sound so bad to you, but I was proud. I didn't feel comfortable paying with food stamps at the local store. I cut a hidden pocket on the inside of my fringed jean jacket so no one caught view of the paper money I had to carry during school. As a matter of fact, I would rather go hungry in school than use my free lunch card. It wasn't uncommon for me to stoop so low as to steal a slice of bread when I got home. I would hide it under my clothes and lock myself in the bathroom and devour it so my mom wouldn't know. We weren't allowed to help ourselves to food just anytime we felt like it; we had to ask for a snack. We were a target for Jehovah's Witnesses too. I felt like we were pitied because we were poor. But those are just some of the reasons there was a passion to owning a beautiful home.

Building a brand-new home on our five acres was a lot of fun. We predetermined where the children's rooms would be someday. We had a friend who was a mason come and mortar the brick for a fireplace. We even had the luxury of a Jacuzzi tub. Some of the perks of marrying a plumber was, he could put these extras in for just the cost of material. We had a large rear deck with atrium doors off the office. This was a house we could experiment on. Not that Herb knew how to tile floors, but he would tackle anything at least once. We didn't know you shouldn't attempt to install tile in freezing temperatures. The next day, most of the tiles popped up, so Herb had to reinstall them. It was a grueling task but a labor of love. My favorite part of the home was our front porch. It was picture perfect, finished off with tan siding and maroon shutters.

We hosted a house-warming party and requested guests that if they wished to bring a gift, we would prefer a meaningful perennial from their own garden. We had most of the items you would need for a home from our accumulation over the years; there really wasn't anything we needed. We just wanted to celebrate the accomplishment we were finally able to achieve. It was a dream come true. Or so we thought.

Back to the time when Dad passed away, Herb's brother Keith was seeing a girl for a while from high school. She was a cheerleader, had reddish-brown hair, a pronounced nose, and beautiful green eyes. Her name was Rita. When they broke off, we kept in touch with her and eventually became good friends with both her and her husband. We were welcomed to be in their wedding ceremony. Their group of friends and family eventually became ours. Rita was outgoing and obnoxious. She was a wild one! She liked to party and drank like a fish. She had a strong, competitive personality and a heart for the handicapped. We used to go up to their hunting cabin and snowmobile and listen to the Steve Miller Band and the Eagles. Sometimes we would head south to the Rhode Island clubs. Most times I blacked out and couldn't remember how ridiculously embarrassing I was. We looked out for each other. Us females had the buddy system in place if we needed to use the restroom in large mobs of people. It was dark and crazy times. I was grateful that Rita's husband would stay sober and drive us looneys around. This arrangement worked out nicely. I never had to volunteer to be the designated driver. I'm not sure if we brought the best out of each other. She had an aggressive personality, and even though we were really close, I got the sense she might have been a bit jealous of me. Maybe we were jealous of each other.

We headed up the long drive north to Maine with a group of nine. We had never gone white water rafting before. It sounded adventurous. We booked a tour on the 109-mile-long Penobscot River, which is the second longest river system in Maine and the longest entirely in the state. Being as inexperienced as we both were, don't ask me why we agreed to go on class V rapids, but we did. Ignorance is bliss? There were sections of the river that were class IV and V. Let me give you a brief breakdown.

The International Rating System classifies rapids as follows:

- Class A: lake water, still
- Class I: easy
- Class II: moderate
- Class III: moderately difficult
- Class IV: difficult
- Class V: extremely difficult
- Class VI: extraordinarily difficult (you're *crazy* in my opinion!)

Class V rapids are extremely long violent rapids and very dangerous. If I may make a suggestion? Don't get on a raft if you get motion sickness, have a weak stomach, or if you drank too much tequila the night before. We couldn't help but laugh at Chris. He wasn't able to hold it in and barfed over the side of our yellow tube into the water. Disgusting!

The rafting guide seemed confident (which I was grateful for). He instructed our group and briefed us on all the rules and what we were to expect. He reiterated the importance of not losing our paddles, which kind of disturbed me. I was more concerned for my life than a paddle that happens to get swept away by the waves of the rapids. We took all safety precautions and fastened on our bright-yellow life jackets and helmets. I thought it was a bit bizarre when Rita brought along her red inflatable shark for the trip (maybe it was for added entertainment purposes). The tour took hours, and we stopped alongside the banks of the river for lunch. So far, so good. No capsizing or drama like I expected with this rowdy group. The bottom of the river was much more intense. We came across a pocket of water that the guide was familiar with. He asked all of us who would like to volunteer for a demonstration. I raised my hand like most of us did. I was the chosen one, lucky me. He told me to situate myself to the front of the raft and hold on to the ropes. I guess the goal was, while I pull the lines, our raft was supposed to "bump" the nose of the boat in the corner of the current and be pushed out backward.

That did not go as planned! I was sucked under the front of the raft faster than I could hold my breath, and I was tumbling underwater in circles like clothes in a washing machine. What turned out to be about a minute and a half felt like an eternity! The scary part was, even though I had a life jacket on, I wasn't coming up to the surface. The strong force of the waves plunged me under like a ragdoll. I remember feeling like I was in slow motion, a bad dream just hoping to wake up. My thoughts were, *I don't even know which way to swim!* Up was nowhere to be found. I hoped I wouldn't slam into a boulder or get hitched underneath by the rocks. Adrenaline was my friend. I didn't have the ability to save myself, and no one came to my rescue. All I could see was a cloak of darkness, and all I could hear was the sound of furious waters. I was afraid to die.

As soon as I couldn't hold my breath any longer, I popped up to the surface and floated. I brawled with the invisible and was fatigued. As I was recovering from what just happened, all I could hear was Rita screaming for me to grab her blow-up shark. I was so perturbed. Give me a break, I could care less about a stupid blow-up at that point; I was just relieved to be in one piece! Later Herb did mention he was nervous when I got sucked up by the river. The guide reassured Herb with perfect precision where and when I was going to pop up. That did give me some consolation.

There were times in our marriage when we were getting sloppy. You tend to take each other for granted when you are best friends. You can assume that even if temptation comes knocking on your door, your will and the will of your partner would be stronger than the desire to throw it all away. Herb and I made a pact that we would never cheat on each other. We would break off with each other first. We saw too many people we cared about in divorce who suffered such devastating betrayal. That wasn't ever going to happen with us. As difficult as it would be to break up, we felt it would be irreparable if one of us cheated on each other. It was one of the worst unforgivable sins in our eyes.

It was just another long weekend in the cabin with our friends. I chopped off my long hair for a shorter style and felt unattractive. I was very insecure in general about myself. We played drinking games and were partying as usual. I always had a desire to share my singing voice with others but rarely could if I was sober. One guy sat there at the table and seemed to appreciate my voice. He gave me a few compliments and asked me to sing him a lullaby. I was flattered by the attention. When it was time for everyone to hit the hay, I refused to join my husband, even though he asked me to go upstairs with him. This guy and I stayed up till the wee hours of the morning and spent time talking and flirting. He was single. He had nothing to offer me, yet I found myself attracted to him. That in and of itself was confusing to me. I loved my husband, so why was I falling for some random guy?

We decided to go to the grocery store in town and pick up some food to make everyone breakfast. When Herb woke up the next morning, he wasn't exactly thrilled that I didn't come to bed. We made an early exit and talked the whole drive home. I felt bad that I behaved the way I did. Even though I didn't cheat in any way sexually, I still had a sense of guilt. I admitted to my honey that I felt like something was wrong in our relationship. I explained to him that I did have "feelings" for this stranger. Herb couldn't believe what he was hearing. He was livid that I would even entertain a "loser" like him. My intentions weren't to hurt my husband. I wanted to just be honest so we could fix what was broken before it was too late. Looking back on this moment, I believe it was courageous that I shared these emotions with my husband. I'm so thankful for the way he responded. He had all the right to be a jerk. He could have dumped me then, but he showed me grace and even admitted some of his own shortcomings. Similar scenarios happened to him in his drinking past. We chose to forgive and vowed to protect what we had. God's hand of divine intervention must have been on us.

After living there at the Cape for a few years, we were struggling. Why were we so unsatisfied? Why were we still empty? What were we missing? Why were we so discontent? There was a moment we both looked out of our bedroom window to the back forest and knew we weren't home. Our heart was still on the land that was promised to us. It was depressing. After all this effort and work, we were still unhappy and unfulfilled.

a Matter of Principle

A good man leaves an inheritance to his children's children.

—Proverbs 13:22 NKJV

We refused to settle for anything less than the one acre of land that Dad promised us. It didn't feel like an inheritance anymore. It was more like a business proposition. We didn't care if we had one acre of unbuildable swampland; we wanted that one acre. It was a matter of principle. We fought hard for almost ten years, but we were determined to make it happen. We pursued our options and concluded that we needed to sell our house in Brookfield. The market was strong, and the newer house was in great condition. The home value increased because we added a two-car garage. We profited well. After all our bills and debts were paid, we had about eighty thousand dollars left. We did run into septic issues that needed to be resolved before we sold the house. I admit Madam Jean did enter my mind, but I just dismissed it as a strange coincidence.

After much negotiating, we were finally able to reach a decision with Herb's mother and brothers. There was only one buildable lot left (due to frontage regulations) and the existing old house; the circumstances were less than ideal. The options were dismal because there were three sons, but only two would be able to benefit from the land. We were appreciative that Mom accepted our offer of twenty thousand dollars for eleven acres of land. Sean would work out a deal to purchase the old house from her with the remaining nine acres. Keith showed no motivation or interest in building. He didn't have a dependable income and would not be able to afford paying for the land anyway. He was basically bought out. We offered him some cash and a newer four-wheel-drive Ford Ranger pickup truck that was paid in full, totaling a value of over ten thousand dollars. Sean worked something out with Keith as well. We used the profit from the sale of the house in Brookfield to purchase, subdivide, and survey the land. We had the land perc-ed and began the foundation with the remainder of the funds. The rest of the home was financed with a construction loan.

We spared no expense since we planned on living there for the rest of our lives. We figured in for a large front porch with a palladium window that centered above our master bathroom. The roof shingles were light brown, and the exterior was finished off with woodland green siding. We envisioned large holiday gatherings when we drew up the plans for the open kitchen, dining room, and living room. We figured in for two bedrooms, three bathrooms, an office, and a huge master bedroom. The house was spacious, well over three thousand square feet. The new house stood close to the very spot that we originally pointed to back when we were teens. It was quite a lengthy process. The septic design was massive and incurred additional unforeseen costs to the project. I was disappointed when we had to haul in more dirt because the ground level became much higher than we were expecting. I always envisioned my front porch landing on ground level, but now we had several stairs to climb for the main entrance. It would take us months to build the home. For a final personalized touch, we pressed our hands in the wet concrete and carved in the year with the words "Dream come true."

* * * * *

You know when you drive by a place, sometimes you wonder what the interior looks like? I've done that many times, especially with old historical houses. There was a white colonial with black shutters and a bright-red door after the center of Main Street in Spencer that was called the Red Maple Inn. It was an old bed-and-breakfast. I used to imagine what kind of antiques and furnishings were inside. It often got my attention when we would pass by. Herb surprised me and told me he worked out a trade bargain in exchange for some plumbing labor with the owners for a month's stay! How cool was that? While we were in the process of building, we needed a place to stay. The Cape didn't take long to sell. We had the privilege of staying in one of the nicest bed-and-breakfasts in town. Being a plumber's wife had its perks!

I was not disappointed when we walked through the doors of that place. The owners did a spectacular job of decorating. Each room had its own theme. Hand-painted murals adorned the walls. There were several oriental rugs, fine china, creaky wide-plank floors, elaborate fireplaces, crown molding, white lace valances, and hand-stitched quilts—it was so beautiful! Even the toilet paper was decoratively folded. The outdoors had wooden Adirondack chairs and plenty of seating that invited guests to relax. The lawn was immaculate. Behind the nearby hostas, there was a birdbath and other scattered perennials throughout the landscape.

During a time when you think I'd be ecstatic, life would throw another curveball. I got news that my mom was very sick. She was suffering for a while, and her symptoms were getting impossible to ignore. When we went to the endocrinologist, my mom was diagnosed with Graves' disease. The doctor told me basically she had one foot in the grave. It weighed heavy on me. Even though we didn't always see eye to eye, I loved her very much. A lot of forgiveness took place between the both of us, and I wanted to be there for her. The doctor suggested she have her thyroid removed. I was dead set against that so-called remedy. I believed the solution could be found with proper nutrition and rest. I had faith she could even be healed. My mom took great pride in her independence. It was a great accomplishment that she could take care of her home on her own, but she was missing work often and becoming weaker and more exhausted. She was holding down a job as a custodian at a school. It was a laborious position. She had good work ethics. She still lived in my childhood home in Charlton that I described earlier. The house was in much better condition. My Memere and Pepere helped her renovate the house and even added a second story. It was unfortunate, but I wasn't there long enough in my teens to actually enjoy the fruits of their labor.

We had nothing but good intentions. Herb understood the severity of my mom's health, and we agreed to offer her a place to stay. She was very reluctant to make the decision to sell her home, but in all fairness, I don't know how she would have been able to keep it if she wasn't able to support herself. We offered to build her an in-law suite attached to our proposed home. We added my mom's roughly eight hundred square feet to the blueprints and got the approval from the town. She would have a small bedroom facing the back deck, a bathroom with her own Jacuzzi tub, and a little kitchenette and living room. I made every promise I could to persuade her to join us. I pretty much begged her to move in with us because I wanted her to live. Graves' disease is a very serious autoimmune condition. Again I was desperate. I watched Herb's father die; I didn't want to go through the loss of my mother too. Herb used to help shovel and plow out my mom when he could. This arrangement would make things a bit easier for us too. Herb wouldn't have to go out to Charlton and shovel or plow her out of the snow anymore, and we would be able to see each other regularly. I could invite her over for dinners, and I imagined her spending quality time with her future grandchildren. Even though Herb and I suffered the loss of two babies, we didn't give up on the idea of having children.

I fantasized we could live like the Waltons. Who doesn't know *The Waltons*? I loved when we used to watch that television series when we were younger. It was based on the life of a Depression-era family in the Blue Ridge Mountains of Virginia that is narrated from the perspective of the oldest son, John Boy. I loved all the characters, especially the grandfather, Zeb. He was funny. This God-fearing family had two loving parents, seven children, and grandparents that lived under the same roof. They enjoyed the simple way of life. They worked hard, had good morals, and even though they were not wealthy, they were rich with love. The women helped each other out in the kitchen, and the children had an innocence. Their home was set in the country with long dirt roads and the house had three dormers and a large front porch, just like the one we were building. I wanted a large family that would help one another out during tough times. I hoped for a bunch of kids and maybe even someday to live off the land. Yeah, and a farm with lots of animals and gardens. I really loved the idea. Why not? I can still hear the loud sound of the trumpet to the theme song of *The Waltons* playing in my mind.

Herb had been self-employed now for a while. He opened a small plumbing and heating business. He was tired of lining everyone else's pockets with his hard labor. He was a journeyman plumber and would continue his education to become a master plumber. A master plumber could make a substantial amount more than a journeyman. I was so proud of him when he passed his test. It didn't come easy for him. He hated taking tests and was more of a hands-on learner, not an academic. I supported him and would eventually learn the basics of owning our own business. It was rewarding becoming your own boss, but also very stressful. People don't call you with good news typically. They call you twenty-four hours a day, seven days a week. There's no nine to five hours in this profession, and usually it's an emergency. When someone has no running water or there was a no-heat call in a blizzard, you can't just ignore them or refer them to someone else, especially when you're starting out. You want to build a dependable reputation and a good name for yourself. We didn't need to advertise much. Most of the work we got were referrals from other satisfied customers. Word of mouth, as they call it.

The service industry of a plumbing business is completely different than a restaurant. When someone orders a burger, they know the price beforehand. They can see the exact amount it will cost right on the menu. Not the case for this kind of work. It's an hourly wage plus material costs. Unfortunately, plumbers have an unpleasant reputation of taking advantage of people, which can make it very difficult to give an invoice to an unsuspecting victim of a broken water pipe. They are usually unhappy before they even get the bill. It's not fun waiting and hoping after you've completed the work if you're going to be compensated for time and material; in some cases, we waited months. And sometimes that would cause us to be late with paying our own bills. It was a difficult, stressful cycle. Some months were really profitable while others were a threat to becoming an employee for someone else. Herb had a heart for the downtrodden too, especially for single moms and the elderly. There were many times he would either give a reduced price or completely absolve the bill. He earned the nickname "Honest Herb," which was quite an accomplishment in this field.

I stayed full-time at the bank, mainly to help cover the cost for health insurance. The money I made helped with a few small bills and groceries. One month went by fast. We had to move on from the Red Maple Inn. Sean was gracious to allow us to stay at the old house while we were in the process of building. It was exciting to watch the house in all its transformations. Little by little, progress was being made. We were anxious to move in; it was rewarding to witness our lifelong dream finally become a reality. We held on to the old proverb "all good things come to those who wait." The construction was impressive to watch. First, the studs would go up, then the trusses. The plywood was nailed and insulation installed. Next would be the roofing, siding, and gutters. The windows were perfectly placed with precision, electrical was wired, plumbing was plumbed, fixtures hung, drywall screwed up, plaster smoothly spread. The final touches of fresh paint, PERGO flooring laid down, trim added, and then the assembly of our hickory kitchen cabinets. Last step was to haul in the appliances and obtain the occupancy permit after final inspections were made. The sound of nail guns and circular saws were music to my ears! I was fond of the smell of fresh sawdust.

We weren't the only ones who moved into Sean's house. Sean's girlfriend Jackie and her son Jacob (who was no older than a toddler) moved in shortly after we did. It was fun to have a little one in the house again. This handsome blue-eyed, blond-haired little tyke was a joy. He used to come upstairs to greet us in the morning. I think his mom thought he was a bother to us; she would tell him to come back downstairs. But really, he was no bother at all. He snuggled with a small brown worn-out stuffed animal that he would call Bear-bear. He didn't demand much attention and was usually well behaved.

Jackie was pretty. She had bleach-blonde hair, beautiful blue eyes with glued-on lashes, and an attractive petite figure. She liked to primp in the mirror a little longer than necessary. I don't believe she knew how beautiful she was naturally. She was often referred to as Barbie because almost every item in her closet was a shade of pink:

light pink, hot pink, bubblegum pink—pink! Every pair of shoes she owned had a five-inch heel, even her platform sneakers. She also had the musical gift for playing piano. It wasn't as quiet now that we had additional people living in the large old house. Nonetheless, I was able to get along with her just fine. She was the girl next door. Her mom owned a horse farm up the road. She was the daughter of an ENT (ears, nose, and throat) doctor. She was a natural with animals. She had a furry companion female dog named Tanner.

Let the Good Times Roll

A friend loves at all times, and a brother is born for a time of adversity.

—Proverbs 17:17 NIV

Some people come into your life for a major purpose, and some are there for a season. Let me introduce you to a man named Patrick. His qualities are fun to describe. He was a single man and a bit peculiar. He wasn't your stereotypical carpenter. He was a carpenter who looked more like a cowboy with his Western hat and boots, turquoise jewelry, and a ruby earring in his ear. He reminded me of the cartoon character Yosemite Sam. He was a steadfast worker, and his choice of music didn't match his persona. He listened to classical music, which drove me nuts! He was a cheerful fella. You couldn't see beyond his freckles; there were so many. He had red peppered hair even on his mustache and beard. Patrick had the physical characteristics of one who is of Irish descent. He loved to talk and describe everything in full detail with his hands. He enjoyed gourmet coffee, red meat, and cigars. He was loyal and old-school. He would tell us tales from his drinking days and share stories about how crazy he was. His laugh was distinctive. He was a likable man.

Herb did some plumbing for the contractor Patrick was working for. The contractor was slow on work, so Herb asked him if he could hire Patrick to do some work for us. Proper etiquette in this line of business is not to hire someone from underneath the original contractor. The contractor arrogantly said that Patrick "belonged" to him. He was disrespectful and cocky. He insinuated that Patrick was his slave. Herb couldn't believe the way he was treating his worker.

Herb lost it and gave the contractor a few choice words. From that day forward, we hired Patrick to work for us full-time.

Patrick wasn't a man who was afraid to cry. He was an emotional guy. He expressed his gratitude when we loaned him some funds upfront so he could purchase a truck. We even let him borrow our truck so he could visit family out of state. He referred to us as the most Christian-like non-Christians he has ever met. We started a new tradition that we would try to bless someone who may not be able to afford Christmas. Annually, we gave one hundred dollars to a stranger anonymously. Patrick told us of a woman at his church who was an artist, and she was going through hard times. She would be the one we would choose to help that year. Patrick's face lit up when we asked him to pass on to her the white envelope full of cash.

Do you remember the motley bunch I worked with at the bank? Over time, the bond of friendships would grow. We would casually go out for drinks and lunches and eventually develop strong ties with their significant others as well. Our group was full of laughter and a lot of fun. We picked on one another often and were guilty of pranking too. Every month, there was a promotion that we were able to put some of our creative energy to use. One year, we dressed up for Halloween as the Flintstones. My boss was Fred, Holly was dressed as Wilma with large white pearls draped around her neck, and Ray made a perfect Bamm-Bamm. The lady with a Brazilian accent was Betty, and from the bright-red hair spray and bone in my ponytail, it was obvious I was Pebbles. I became persuasive from my cross-selling techniques that I even convinced all my coworkers to pitch in and buy the new book of ten-dollar scratch tickets that just made their debut. Ten people gambling one hundred dollars each. Minimal risk for a potentially high prize. I was hoping we would win a huge jackpot; we didn't. Christmas parties were the most memorable. Usually Holly and her husband, Ryan, would host the gathering in their nice home in Hubbardston. Holly carried a tune well, and Ryan could play the drums. They were both musically talented.

Ray was a good kid. I really liked his girlfriend. She seemed to be his perfect match. I'm pretty sure I encouraged him some when he was planning on proposing to her. They were cute together and in love. She had beautiful thick, long wavy auburn hair. She was short like me and had large light-brown eyes. Her name was Misty. It was hard not to laugh when she would because if she really thought something was funny, she had an uncontrollable snorting sound. Misty was a girl with strong conviction. If her opinion didn't agree with your philosophy, she didn't hesitate to express herself. She had no problem with confrontation. She was feisty. Aerosmith doesn't have a truer fan. She knew every word to all their songs. Even though she loved Steven Tyler, I think she had a thing for Joe Perry, the lead guitarist. They reminded me a lot of Herb and I when we were younger. They were just starting out and had so many aspirations. They were planning on getting married and wanted to move in together. We didn't have many couples we looked up to when we were starting out; we wanted them to have a fighting chance. We found ourselves putting them under our wing. We wanted to help them succeed.

Herb and I talked it over and offered them a place to stay in our basement. Our house was huge, and we had a lot of additional space that we didn't really use. Besides, how cool would it be to have friends close by? They eagerly agreed, and we began finishing off our basement. Ray and Misty would help by picking the colors and painting the walls before they moved in. We gave them a small kitchenette, a bathroom, and a tiny bedroom and living room (they would later call their bevingroom), which was basically just enough space for a couch. We loved having them. They were the kind of people who seemed to really appreciate and respect us. We all got along well. They pitched in to help with a portion of the household expenses. They weren't there for a free ride, and they didn't take advantage. We always felt included in their lives. We felt like family.

It was so much fun watching them plan for their wedding. Misty chose a beautiful white wedding gown with blue sapphire stones that wrapped around the side. She trusted me to help her with her makeup, and I was honored to be her bridesmaid, along with her sisters. She had a navy-blue dress for the girls. Ray invited Herb to be a groomsman. We surprised them with a pair of white doves at the wedding. Misty mentioned how she wished she could have them on her wedding day. We felt so accepted and included as part of their families. As a joke, I questioned if Misty and Ray would like us to join them on their honeymoon to Aruba. I told them we didn't have an extravagant honeymoon because we were so young and low on funds. Even though I thought it was tacky, we needed to throw a greenback shower to help pay for our wedding. A greenback shower is a practical way to help the couple foot the bill for their wedding. We invited nearly 250 people. That is why we only had about six hundred dollars left for Bar Harbor, Maine. I would have preferred some warm tropical island if I had a choice. The night of their wedding, Tim and his girlfriend were the only responsible adults who reserved a hotel room. We, along with other friends, drank too much and crashed their hotel room for the night. Us and the doves.

Understandably, Ray and Misty said no way, we weren't going to hitch a ticket and spoil their romantic getaway. Then they gave it a second thought and reconsidered, just in case they might need someone to bail them out of jail on foreign soil—they always had such a great sense of humor! Of course, we would be honored to bail them out! So we headed on a plane, the four of us, for some rest and relaxation. White sandy beaches and predictable sunny climates, the trade winds gave a cool steady breeze from the northeast and kept the island comfortable even though daily temperatures were in the high eighties. The divi-divi trees are native to the Caribbean and bordered the island throughout. They were majestic and looked like a bonsai tree. The branches all lean toward the same side and are well known to help you navigate your way to town. Even the license plates said "One Happy Island." For breakfast, we would roll out of bed and have a cocktail at the beach bar. We stayed at the all-inclusive resort called the La Cabana. It was one of my favorite vacations.

Herb and Ray dared each other to eat ostrich burgers. I was less gutsy. You couldn't pay me enough to eat an ostrich! One of the many amusing times was when Herb and Ray went together for a luxury massage. Here you have two young clueless men on a strange island far away from Massachusetts believing some attractive Aruban goddesses was going to pamper them with fragrant oils. They were both in their birthday suits covered only by white linen towels with their faces perfectly fit into a doughnut-shaped pillow with just enough vision to see the floor as they lay facedown. The two professional licensed therapists were less than attractive. One was an older heavyset masseuse (a woman), and the other was a thin hairy man with large hands (the man), a masseur. As Herb was peering down through the opening of his doughnut pillow, he recognized the woman's shoes. He was very relieved to get the female. Yes, I'm laughing out loud—you had to be there! Herb and Ray looked like two vulnerable victims instead of two happy customers. Ray, unfortunately, could tell by his limited view as he looked down onto the floor that he had the hairy man. You could tell by his comment to Herb he was displeased. He warned Herb (since he was the one who got the man) that he better never tell a word to anyone! Ray must not have been too upset; at one point, Herb noticed Ray even fell asleep!

We enjoyed high-end restaurants, shopping, snorkeling, and a very bumpy off-road jeep excursion. Herb was at the wheel of that Jeep rental. He lost the tour guide on purpose and drove like a maniac. We felt more like hostages by his lead foot on the dusty stone landscape. I'm pretty sure we didn't escape without body bruises from that intense ride. We also went horseback riding, which was something I always wanted to experience. Trust me, it was less than exotic. I envisioned us as a couple peacefully riding horseback along the shorelines of the sea, just like something from the Hallmark Channel. Nope, it was far from the tourist brochures they hand you at the hotel desk. I was scared to death! On horseback, we were climbing rocky terrain on the steep cliffs of Aruba looking down into the ocean. I didn't know my fear of heights was going to be tested. My horse, like many others on the tour, stopped in her tracks and lay down right in the sand. We laughed hysterically when we noticed Ray and Misty on the private honeymoon tour way ahead of us. They wanted a romantic experience with their own personal guide. We caught a glimpse of Ray being bucked off his horse, and he was plopped right into the ocean waves. He had to walk the rest of the way back to the ranch because his horse ran and deserted him. As far as I was concerned, they should have been able to get their money back!

"Texas hold 'em" was a popular poker game. Herb and I learned how to play cards religiously every week in our garage. What started off as just a few people grew into roughly a couple dozen. I discovered new traits I didn't know I had. I learned the art of healthy competition. I used to get a kick out of being the underdog and winning a hand I had no business keeping. No feeling can compare to holding on to a pair of deuces and getting a full boat on the river! Ah, the sound of raking a win and stacking your chips to your corner of the table was joyous! We even entered large tournaments that had a couple hundred contestants and have actually won! It was rewarding to earn hundreds-of-dollar pots! I reveled when men would underestimate me, and sometimes I would play dumb and bluff my opponents. Most times I could keep my face from revealing my hand. It wasn't often I would pitch my cards to the dealer. I enjoyed showing my hand, whether I had pocket jacks or nothing at all. Betting was intense. You had to really study the people who were playing. Are they risky? Do they appear too excited? Are they talking a lot? Maybe they've been too quiet. Are their faces red with high blood pressure? Are they sweating? Do they keep peeking at their cards? Do they cap their cards a little too tightly? Some of the body language were telltale signs if you should fold or raise a bet. We'd even go to Foxwoods and play for hours there. We would sarcastically joke and claim our retirement funds were invested into Foxwoods Casino. We would go there often, play the tables, or if we wanted to be antisocial, we would sit at the slot machines for hours. My favorite game was Double and Triple Diamonds. Wild Cherries was another fun one.

Ray's younger sister Jenna would become acquainted with Sean's friend John at our weekly poker games. They would fall in love and eventually tie the knot. Gambling became a bit addicting. We would both spend a great amount of our paychecks for a fix. We were thrill seekers. Sometimes I would get a rush if I slapped the "max bet" button and would win. And if we spent more money than we initially agreed on, we would go home feeling defeated, guilty, and regretful. It was an emotional roller coaster. Winning felt fantastic; losing hurt bad. It was another way for us to socialize. It brought us together as family and as friends. Not many people we knew didn't play something. Pick your drug of choice: keno, bingo, cards, or slots.

I would repeat the silliest things: "Mamma needs a brand-new pair of shoes," "Go big or stay home." Or I would rub the side of the slot machine like a magic lamp and pray to the Foxwoods genie to shower me with wealth. Of course, there was no strategy that worked, just a lot of guessing, wishing, and superstition. With slots, the odds of winning were less than probable. I used to just sit there like a zombie and either monotonously pull a lever or effortlessly press a button, then repeat the process. It was almost therapeutic. With all the constant noise and bells ringing, it was like I entered my own world. I could escape reality. You knew I was desperate when I had to use the bathroom facility and would hold the urge to urinate for hours just so I wouldn't lose my machine. Nothing short of an emergency could peel me from my machine. Well, even an emergency wouldn't.

One time, Misty and Ray and a group of friends all decided to go together in the same vehicle. It takes about an hour and a half to get there, so it was nice not always having to drive. Poor Misty wasn't feeling well. I can't say I had a whole lot of sympathy. I selfishly made her wait because I was on a winning streak. By the time we left, we had to pull over so she could get sick. It dawned on me then that I had a problem. I was remorseful, but it was too late. I was thankful she didn't hold a grudge.

I had no pride. Yes, I would stoop low enough to beg my husband for more money. I tried to negotiate with him when I ran out. And if he wouldn't give me more money, I would nag whoever else was with me. I had no self-control. I was even greedy when I won. If I won seven hundred dollars, I wished I won jackpot. I was so dissatisfied.

The casino was like Emerald City. It was massive and almost heavenly. The architecture was impressive; that place was so stimulating to all five senses. We compromised our limitations often when we would visit there. We attempted to protect ourselves by keeping all checks and ATM cards locked at home. All the promises and vows made before we entered that building were scattered in the wind. We lacked restraint. It became a dangerous habit. Not only did it affect our finances, it affected my breathing (I can't begin to tell you how much secondhand smoke I inhaled). It even affected my nerves.

Sometimes a room full of people would cause me great anxiety. I was flustered, whether I won or lost. It would literally take hours for my ears to recover from the loud noises and for my ears to stop ringing. And forget it if I landed pocket aces—the exhilaration caused me bowel problems!

If I lost my allowable portion of spending and had to wait for others that we drove in with, I had nothing better to do than resort to searching the floor for dropped coins. There were moments that I found humorous. Most grandmother-type ladies seemed kind and sweet. Not in a casino! Move over, 'cause Grandma don't seem as innocent as she appears! How one grumpy woman can play three or four slot machines simultaneously takes real skill! She clutched onto her short-handled purse pressed closely by her side and gave the evil glance if you even considered sitting near her machines. Gambling was serious business!

Let's just be honest, shall we? If I wasn't feeling lucky on a slot machine that I had been dumping a lot of money and time into and decided to move to another machine that was close by, I had to grit my teeth and pretend I was happy for the random person who nonchalantly put one coin in my previous machine and won. I swear smokers blew their cigarette smoke in my face on purpose just to get rid of me. I was stubborn to a fault and would just hold my breath under the collar of my shirt. No one was having my machine!

In 2001, I wanted to do something really special for Herb on his twenty-seventh birthday. I asked him if he would like to fulfill one of his crazy dreams of skydiving. Without hesitation, we gathered a handful of his buddies (Ray and his brother being two of them) and started off with breakfast (bold move) and drove to Rhode Island. For a couple hundred bucks, you can get a thrill of a lifetime! I had butterflies, and I wasn't even going on the plane. You could sense the nervousness and adrenaline the guys had. They were so pumped up. This can't compare to waiting in line at Six Flags for a roller coaster; it's far more extreme. There I was, all by myself, standing on top of the picnic table (those couple extra feet didn't get me any closer to the clouds) balling my eyes out. I had such terrible regret. Fear came over me, and I had a bad case of the what-ifs. I had moments to dread: *What if he dies because I bought him this gift? What if he doesn't land right and breaks a leg? What if something goes awfully wrong with the plane? What if the parachute doesn't open?* All I could see was a speck in the sky as small as the size of a dot made by a pencil on a blank piece of paper. That was him. He jumped out of a small plane at ten thousand feet high. According to the VCR tape, he didn't actually jump; he was clipped into his instructor and sat at the edge of the plane door and rolled out backward! What a rush! It averages about two hundred feet per second during a skydive. From ten thousand feet, he was in a free fall for about thirty seconds. A professional photographer took pictures of the entire experience. He was side by side with Herb and his blonde tandem enthusiast. Herb never looked as exhilarated. He had two thumbs up in his pictures with his mouth wide open as gusts of wind were flapping his cheeks. It's a good thing his teeth weren't false. Needless to say, I was relieved when I saw his parachute open and when they both landed safely to the ground. The tape captured every morsel of this memory to the tune of Lenny Kravitz's "Fly Away."

There were a few benefits of not having children yet. We could be irresponsible and frivolous. We threw some extravagant parties. Rarely we did much of anything small. We had such a blast planning my husband's thirtieth birthday party. It is in August, so we decided to host it at our house. We had a lot of space and an open yard for a lot of attendees. The theme was "Herbie Goes Bananas." It was a luau. Every person who arrived was greeted and gifted a beautiful lei. We hired a man to come and entertain us with his real Panamanian white-faced monkey. Her name was Pearl; she was an instant hit! We loved to include our guests and get them involved. We offered a grand prize winner for the best costume. More people participated than didn't. There were many creative costumes. My sister and her friend dressed up as Bob Marley with tie-dye T-shirts and dread locks; they had the whole Rastafarian look down perfectly. Tim was a gnarly surfer dude. Ray was a giant life-sized human banana. Misty and a few of her friends came with a trio of colorful wigs and floral dresses. Herb had a burgundy straw hat with long black braids. He wore a tan hula skirt, floral bracelets, large oversized plastic bare feet, and a coconut bra.

This party took us days to prepare. Herb had an awesome idea to buy a Volkswagen Beetle from the junkyard. He cut it in half, painted it white, and slapped on a decal with the number 53. It wasn't just a decoration. You could pop open the trunk (which is in the front of the car), and voila, you got a cooler for all your beverages.

While the kids were bobbing for apples, the adults were bobbing for nips. We always had something fun for the kids to do. We rented a large inflatable elephant bounce house and had potato-sack races. The adults were having just as much fun as the kids were. Herb and I really enjoyed watching the laughter and smile on people's faces. We took great pleasure in seeing everyone in a blissful state. We invited everyone. No one was excluded. All were welcome—neighbors, friends, and family. And if someone wanted to bring a guest? No problem! The more, the merrier!

We had a lot of people who helped us out too. My uncles Paul and Roy manned the grill, Ray bartended in his banana costume behind the tiki bar, and Lora (Misty's friend) offered to bake the massive cake. She ended up having to leave prematurely. Too much fun too fast, she was intoxicated in less than an hour and had to go home. I felt so bad for her. Been there done that.

Most people use a stick to poke and hit a piñata. Herb could find a solution for just about everything! He could think outside the box. After many attempts of smacking the papier-mâché container full of candies and coins with no success, Herb came to the rescue with the chainsaw and became the hero of the evening.

The disk jockey played all kinds of music: reggae, country, classic rock, you name it. It wasn't unusual for me to pick up the microphone and sing a song or two. Toward the end of the evening, I sang karaoke with a few of our friends. Times don't change much. The police came to let us know our neighbors thought our singing was awful. By the expression on their faces, they weren't too serious. They just asked us if we could keep it down for the sake of our neighbors. Understood. Boy, was I insulted. After a few drinks, I thought we sounded pretty good!

I'd have to say the most exciting scene was in the backyard. We hired an agency to come and give hot-air balloon rides. This grand yellow, red, and black vertically striped balloon was impressive. People patiently waited in long lines to take their turn in the basket. It was tethered to the ground for safety purposes and allowed to lift about fifty feet into the air to give one the general idea of the experience on a hot-air balloon. For a blue-collar worker, this party was above our paygrade. We spent over five thousand dollars on this event. I can honestly say we would do it all over again. We had no regrets. We used to live by the saying "life is too short." When we talk with distant relatives over a decade later, they still refer to that party being one of the best times they ever had. I believe the memories made that day are cherished forever in all who were able to attend. It was worth every penny!

I know some people can't hold their liquor. Our group of friends most times weren't angry or aggressive drunks. They were usually obnoxiously funny and loving. In a world where it's not "manly" to be emotional creatures, I found alcohol to be as powerful as truth serum. You could tell someone's true feelings about certain conversations or people in general. "I love you, man"—I can't tell you how many times I heard the guys express their brotherly affection for one another. It was heart-warming and genuine and acceptable only if you'd been drinking. It would just be awkward or strange if we were sober and said those same exact words.

Getting large groups of people together wasn't hard to do. A lot of our friends had the same interests. Herb missed sports from his high school days and asked the guys if they would like to join him on a softball league. My uncle Mark used to coach my aunt Donna's (his sister's) team years earlier, so he had the experience and was willing to participate. Herb took every opportunity to make others laugh. We ordered black-and-white striped prison uniforms for the softball team. It was like watching a *Three Stooges* episode. We had their numbers and last names printed on the back of their shirts in bright orange. As we watched them run onto the field, they looked like rowdy inmates. One time, a mother clung onto her children and took them to the parking lot to leave. I don't think she realized they weren't true prisoners. Our English bulldog Chopper made the perfect mascot. He even wore his matching inmate tank top. The team won the championship that year.

Even though we loved being an aunt and uncle, having children of our own kind of went on the back burner. It wasn't a priority. We were having too much fun.

The following year, my sister, Keri, and I turned thirty. We held another large celebration, this time at the Spencer Country Inn. The theme was "The Twins Are Turning Thirty and Got the Blues." We repeated similar ideas from Herb's party. Best Costume wins one hundred dollars, and there was a live blues band. We also had it catered. Some of the costumes were well thought out. My honey was a magical wizard. I made his robe from blue velvet that dragged on the floor, and we borrowed a pair of stilts that made Herb tower above everyone at nine feet tall. He bought a long wooden staff and applied makeup to imitate the face of an old man. We glued on eyebrows, a gray mustache, and a long beard on his face. He was not recognizable. I was a fairy. I had blue monarch-butterfly wings edged with black, a lace corset, and a lengthy feminine sheer skirt to match. I found a royal-blue sapphire-gem necklace that I wore as a crown that draped over my forehead. I added long hair extensions, pointy fair-skinned ears, and pale opaque skin that shimmered with body glitter. My twin dressed up as a police officer. Her uniform looked authentic with her crisp blue shirt, shiny black hat, and badge. Ray was Captain America, and Craigy dressed as King Tut. We had Cookie Monster and four Dorothies from *The Wizard of Oz*. Misty had me in stitches as she tried to balance her towering blue bouffant wig; she made the perfect Marge Simpson. Of course, Tim and Ryan came as the Blues Brothers—how appropriate. My brother had the most hilarious costume of all; I have no idea where he found it. He had a mask on of an old redneck man with a white mustache and fuzzy hair, wearing the worst wedgie over the back of his head. His skivvies were blue. Toward the end of the evening, I sang an old Patsy Cline song, "Sweet Dreams," in a light-blue sequin tube dress and later would encourage my younger cousin Erika (while she got up the bravery) to sing a song too.

As our siblings would creep up to thirty, we hosted parties for them as well. Keith loved NASCAR, so we threw a race-car-themed party with black-and-white checkered flags and bought small tricycles with metal bugle horns to race them up and down our long asphalt driveway. I have pictures proving even a very pregnant woman with determination can pedal fast on a child's toy. Sean was into gambling, so that was simple. We rented a Greyhound bus for him, and after the party, we all headed for a long evening at the casino. My brother was a fishing fanatic. We rented a hall, flipped burgers and hot dogs on the barbeque, and set up a tent, collapsible camping chairs, and a fake campfire with marshmallows on sticks. I can remember my nephew fishing with the magnetic fish and pole we set up by the kiddie pool. We even got him his own personal drink cooler that looked like a huge red-and-white floating bobber. The DJ played Brad Paisley's song "I'm Gonna Miss Her" (which is a comical country song about a guy having to choose between his girl or fishing).

It didn't take Ray and Misty long to announce they were expecting their first baby. They were so compassionate and sensitive as they shared the wonderful news. They harnessed their joy because they understood how many years we were trying to conceive. They knew our suffering and didn't want to "rub in" their blessing. Also they wanted us to hear the news straight from their lips. You might think we would have been jealous, but Herb and I were very happy for them. When you go through years of infertility and two miscarriages, the last thing you want is for your close friends to go through the same struggles. Our hearts were warmed when they asked us if we would be the baby's godparents. They were thoughtful and considerate to think of us, and we would be more than happy to receive their offer.

One starry night, we were talking outside on our rear deck discussing life in general. We reflected on our businesses and finances and recognized some changes needed to be made. By this time, we grew our plumbing business into a corporation and had a few employees. There was a lot of maintenance and upkeep, and bills were stacking high. One supply company was owed a whopping sixty thousand dollars. No matter how hard we worked, we just couldn't get out of the red. We were both very aggravated. We wanted things to happen faster. You'd think after accomplishing the decade-old dream home of finally living on his father's land, that would give us some satisfaction. But our appetites were always unsatisfied. I could barely keep up with managing the businesses and the house. I was beside myself when my honey had the audacity to say these two words to me: "I'm bored!"

A Deal with the Devil

But godliness with contentment is great gain. For we brought nothing into the world, and we can take nothing out of it. But if we have food and clothing, we will be content with that. Those who want to get rich fall into temptation and a trap and into many foolish and harmful desires that plunge people into ruin and destruction. For the love of money is a root of all kinds of evil. Some people, eager for money have wandered from the faith and pierced themselves with many griefs.

—1 Timothy 6:6–10 NIV

Do you know the movie *It's a Wonderful Life*? That is one of our favorite Christmas movies of all time. There are many relatable moments for us in that movie. George Bailey is a man of integrity, and he is asked to meet Mr. Henry Potter (a greedy old man). There's a scene where George is given a generous offer to work with his nemesis, and the offer is very appealing. He is lured with an expensive cigar and enticed by the idea of buying his wife fine clothes. Also, George is bribed with a three-year lucrative salary and the possibility of traveling to Europe a couple times a year (which was something he always wished to do). It all sounds like an amazing opportunity. George tells Mr. Potter he's going to go home and talk it over with his wife. As George stands up to shake Mr. Potter's hand, he quickly loses the smile on his face, and he looks at his right hand. Then George wipes his hand on his coat and realizes he was just tempted to sell out all he believes in. He storms out of Mr. Potter's office, refusing the deal. The difference between this character and my husband is even though Herb had a bad feeling, he still went forward against his own better judgement. He was clouded by the fact that the man he shook hands with was his uncle.

There must be a better way. After all the sweat and toil of working strenuously all our lives, we couldn't see ourselves ever getting ahead. We had a lot of debt, a good-sized mortgage, and over five hundred customers to keep happy. No savings, no retirement—we were still living paycheck to paycheck on the downward spiral. The only reason Herb chose plumbing was because his dad suggested it, but to be honest, Herb was burnt out. We knew for a few years Herb's uncle was successful in real estate. We were glad for him because as far back as we could remember, he was seemingly unhappy, unmotivated, and extremely overweight. Now he was at a healthy weight and flaunting his riches to the family. He was a completely different person. More confident, outgoing, and generous. He made offers to Herb in the past, but Herb wasn't interested. We were ripe for the picking. We were young, desperate, and wet behind the ears. This time, when the offer came, we gave it some consideration. We even went to a local attorney to put our fears to rest and proposed the idea to him. The attorney asked us questions on Herb's uncle's methods. We knew very little but explained the process as best as we could. The lawyer told us, "Well, there's no law against it. It's either genius or borderline illegal." He encouraged us because we were still young enough to take risks, and since Herb's uncle had been doing it for a few years without any negative results, the lawyer didn't see a problem if we wanted to give it a try.

That gave us the green light. So Herb and I met one evening at a Dunkin Donuts with his uncle. After a short conversation, Herb agreed to give it a shot. When Herb shook his uncle's hand that night, I felt like he just shook hands with the devil. Something didn't feel right. I don't know if it was intuition, my gut—call it what you want—but I was unsettled and didn't fully understand why. There was a part of me that wanted to trust the man and give him the benefit of the doubt, but another side of me was leery and suspicious.

Herb was eager to begin something new. It was exciting. It felt like he could finally make a living doing something that didn't require his hands to get dirty. We put aside Herb's jeans and work boots and went to the mall to buy a few suits. We got three two-piece suits. One was black, another was striped navy blue, and the third one was camel colored, all tailored to fit. We bought a few ties, dress shirts, and a pair of black Oxfords. It was different and refreshing. No employees, no overhead, just a commission-based pay. Herb had a great reputation. People liked him. When he gave his word, he meant it. He was ambitious and determined to give it all he had.

Herb's uncle invited us to dinner a few times. Once we went to a nice restaurant on Park Avenue, and I can remember indulging myself to Alaskan king crab for the first time. I would never have tried a meal that hefty in price, but we were surrounded by people who had an abundance of wealth. The pressure to fit in was imminent. After we pulled out a plastic credit card to pay for our meal, Herb's uncle offered to treat everyone. I wasn't proud to accept his offer; I was quite relieved. I was astonished when I saw the total amount on the receipt. It was over one thousand dollars for one sitting. That amount would have covered our grocery bill for two months!

The flyers said good news! We believed people were being helped and were given hope. All that needed to be done was to arrange a meeting for Herb's uncle to speak with the person who was in foreclosure. If that person agreed, then Herb would receive a commission for his time. We noticed a few odd things right away at the office. Some of the people seemed shady. One day when Herb was out working, I was in the office, and an irate man came barging through the office door demanding to see Herb's uncle. He had a gun. I can remember calling Herb from my cell phone in my car explaining what just happened and that I wanted to be done. I was nervous and pleaded with him that this risk was not worth our lives. I wanted some answers. Why was this angry man looking for his uncle? How many more enemies did he have? What in the world did we get ourselves into? It felt like a scene from a mob movie, but this was real life. Even though it all appeared to be legitimate, I kept my guard up. I believed if we did everything aboveboard and as long as we were honest, we would be okay. I made deposits in large sums at our bank without reservation. I didn't have anything to hide, and I claimed every penny on taxes.

It wasn't until one of the people who worked with his uncle pulled us aside and whispered to us that we seemed like really nice people. He suggested we get out while we can. He informed us that

Herb's uncle was being investigated by the FBI. He was believable. He warned us that even though we were innocent, we could be considered guilty by association. He knew the law. He also was an attorney. We hastily took heed of the man's advice and immediately moved our desks and belongings. We didn't need to be told twice. When Herb confronted his uncle, he defended himself and confessed that he was, in fact, working *with* the FBI. He tried to convince us that the rumors were false. He swore over his brother's grave (Herb's father) that he would never put us in harm's way and that there was absolutely nothing to worry about. Even though we wanted to believe him, it was all a lie. And now it was too late.

Never did we think when we came home that we would be greeted with a three-million-dollar attachment on our home. Herb was served papers that named him as one of the dozens of defendants of a major civil lawsuit. We were in disbelief and shock. How could this happen? The most trouble Herb ever got into was a measly speeding ticket. Herb never had any run-ins with the law before. What does all this mean? Jail? Immediately we called that attorney whom we saw previously for advice, and he told us he didn't represent civil cases and would refer us to someone he knew. He reassured us that he would put in a good name for us. *Scared* doesn't fully describe the emotion we were suffering from. Innocent until proven guilty? That is not how this game works. Herb was guilty until we could pay to prove otherwise. Even though the battle took years, it would cost us everything!

The first thing we did was look for an attorney to represent Herb. We scanned the yellow pages and found a guy who agreed to help us if we gave him a $1,600 retainer. We scraped up the money and went to his office to give him all the proper documents. He neglected us big-time. He sat on our paperwork for weeks and denied us the opportunity to be reimbursed. He was a fraud. We had a deadline to make with no attorney. We were scrambling for resources, desperate for help, and we were losing hope fast.

We met another attorney who was part of a large firm in Worcester. His name was Dan Mulaney, thanks to the referral from the first attorney we originally sought advice from. As far as I was concerned, the least he could do was point us in the right direction since he gave us poor advice. You'd think he would have told us to back off or stay away from this uncle. Even though no one twisted our arm to make the decision to get involved, he sure could have steered us away from something this dangerous. We played with fire and got burnt. Severely.

We were relieved when this young attorney took on the case. He had a lot of questions and really couldn't believe how naive we were. He asked us for a significantly large retainer. I pulled out stacks of cash to pay him. Right there and then, I realized it just didn't look good. He asked me why I had so much cash on hand. I told him as soon as this all came crashing down on us, I pulled all our money out of the bank because I didn't know if there would be a levy or hold on our accounts. I explained this was all we had left and how afraid we both were.

Dan told us he wouldn't even consider taking on this case if it wasn't for the referral he got. He was told that we were young kids who got into a heap of trouble and needed help. That we were good kids. He accepted us out of sheer pity. For that, I was grateful. I've never been reprimanded by an attorney before. I can remember Herb trying to explain how this all began. Dan would get so frustrated with us because we should have seen the signs. Even though he was professional, he was also human. He would get very passionate with us. His famous line was, "If it doesn't pass the smell test, then it's probably bad!" Sometimes we just felt so stupid. When the lawyer would use his lingo and verbiage, we had a hard time understanding half the conversation. Once he could tell for himself that we really had the best intentions and that we believed what Herb's uncle told us, I could tell Dan believed us. He invested a lot in us. He was consumed by this long, miserable court battle. There were times I felt so sorry for all the trouble this was causing our attorney. This wasn't an easy one. It was complicated.

I can remember one time when Herb had to go into a room full of lawyers and give a deposition. A deposition is a process of giving sworn evidence. It's a question-and-answer session where opposing counsel asks you questions to learn more about your case. A court reporter records your testimony with a stenography machine and then creates a written transcript to be used at trial. It was stressful, and no matter how much Herb prepared for it, he was never quite fully prepared. My husband had to answer questions literally for seven hours. It was mentally and emotionally draining.

Having the same last name with the uncle that's responsible for mortgage schemes didn't help. Many of the victims not only went after the uncle for compensation but came after Herb. They wanted to get compensated for their losses (rightfully so) and would go to any length to get it. My poor husband wasn't just fighting one lawsuit; he had a few. Every time he passed by the front door to our home, he would break out in a cold sweat. Fear would overcome him. The threat of another lawsuit or the sight of another deliverer handing him papers was too hard to handle. It's pretty sad when even the constable is familiar with our doorstep and spoke to Herb and told him how badly he felt for him.

We couldn't keep up with the legal fees. We were paying tens of thousands for top-of-the-line representation. I remember a goal Herb had. By the time he turned thirty, he wanted to be a millionaire. We certainly weren't millionaires yet, but we had a lot of real estate. Over time, those rentals would have been worth a conservative million. Our portfolio was diminishing. We didn't have assets or cash. But we had equity. Slowly it was chipping away, and there was absolutely nothing we could do about it. We couldn't sell any of our properties because there were attachments on them. We were sitting ducks. All we could do was max out the equity on our dream home. We were ordered to put in a septic system on our lake-house property as one of the conditions to appease the plaintiff. We did. But we lost even more tens of thousands.

I was disappointed when one of my family members who was renting a property of ours stopped paying us. He could see the house was probably going into foreclosure and planned on staying for a few months rent-free to save for first, last, and security of his next place. All the while, we had to still cover costs out of our own pocket. The walls were crashing down hard. Our marriage was taking a toll. We were hitting rock bottom. No one could help us, and there was nowhere to turn. We were broken.

amazing Grace

But I will call on God, and the Lord will rescue me. Morning, noon, and night I cry out in my distress, and the Lord hears my voice. He ransoms me and keeps me safe from the battle waged against me, though many still oppose me.

—Psalm 55:16–18 NLT

Times were difficult enough with the lawsuit constantly threatening us. The last thing I expected was more tragedy. As I was growing up as a child, my mom's family was very close. We used to get so excited when our cousins would come over to visit and play together with us. Not that it was fair to pick favorites, but I know we all did. Some bonds were closer than others.

I remember one evening around six o'clock. I felt a heavy weight come over me. I told Herb I was going to bed. I was a night owl, but something depleted my energy. It was unusual for me to unplug my phone, but I didn't want to be disturbed. I slept through the entire night, and when I woke, I received a phone call from my sister, Keri, that our cousin Jessika died from fentanyl poisoning. It was two days before her nineteenth birthday. Trauma and shock set in. At first, I was numb. I had a million questions, and my heart hurt for the whole family.

I thought back to the last time I saw her. She came to visit my mom next door. I remember toward the last days of her life, she struggled a lot. She knocked on a lot of doors, but I didn't know how to help her. She wasn't the kind of girl that you could even picture using drugs—how could this happen? She truly was a brilliant, athletic, talented, humble, and kind soul. She wasn't rebellious. She wasn't a troublemaker. She was one of seven siblings. She didn't fit the description of someone with addiction problems. I had a lot of regret. Almost always do I make it a point to address my loved ones with affection. I'm a huge hugger, and most of us always say "I love you" at the end of a visit. But for whatever reason that day, when she came, I didn't make the effort to squeeze her like I normally would. Then she decided to go next door to visit with Sean and Jackie. I assumed I would be able to catch up with her later. That never happened. Did she feel disapproval by me? Did she feel ashamed or judged or criticized? I'm not so sure. But what I do know is, when a life is stolen away from you that quickly, it changes everything—the way you treat others, the way you view life, if there is anyone you need to say sorry to. I wondered, *Where is she right now? Is she in heaven? Is she alive in another dimension? Is she at peace? Is she finally happy? Did she know I loved her?* (Sadly, her older brother Jeremy would die from the same addiction nearly eleven years later.)

One of my favorite pictures of us together is when we were both bridesmaids for Sean and Jackie's wedding. We were all dolled up in satin black-and-white chiffon gowns facing each other. My Auntie Judy often took pictures of the family; she was able to capture a special moment. We were standing outside near velvety green meadows at the Spencer Country Inn. There were gorgeous stone walls, and the trees were in full bloom. To the common onlooker, we probably look serious as we were posing hand in hand. Her face reflected the sunset. Truth is, I loved to tease her and make her laugh. I was pretending to propose to her. We both have this smile on our faces as we are gazing into each other's eyes. That's how I want to remember her. I hope one day she will greet me in paradise the same way with her arms extended to me, her face radiating, and welcome me with her beautiful smile. You can be sure I will give her the biggest hug when that day comes.

The best thing about learning a trade was, it was always something you could fall back on. We needed to support ourselves, so Herb dusted off his tools and began looking for work. It's all he knew. It surely wasn't his preference, but it might keep our necks above water for the time being. What's that saying? Beggars can't be choosers?

Do you remember our good ole carpenter friend Patrick? He was helping Ray and Misty build their new home just a few houses up from ours. The small apartment was getting cramped with baby accessories. Ray and Misty gave up their bedroom for the baby and made their living room their "bevingroom." Herb noticed Pat was behaving a bit odd. The biggest thing Herb noticed was, he wasn't swearing anymore. What was up with this guy? Something was different. Patrick mentioned the church he was attending was praying for God to supply them with a reputable plumber. The job was quite substantial. Herb needed to look at the job and what it entailed so he could give an estimate. I rode with him that day. When we pulled into the parking lot, I can remember thinking, *This is a church?* It didn't really look like one. From what I recollect, it used to be an old lumberyard. They basically just painted it green and added a steeple to it.

I told Herb I did not want to get out of the truck. Churches weren't a comfortable place for me. I was very unsociable, especially with the drama we were in the middle of. My sense of confidence had dwindled significantly. Patrick introduced Herb to the pastor of the church. From my quick assessment, the pastor had my approval. He looked like a normal guy wearing a pair of jeans. He was down to earth, and I was relieved to hear he had a wife. (No offense, but after all the negative publicity with the priests, I was all set with a celibate man in robes).

We were relieved to hear that the church approved our quote and was ready for the work to begin. Patrick asked us if we would like to check out his church with him on Sunday. I thought maybe it wouldn't hurt to go to a church service. We needed something; we tried everything else that we could think of. We got up the nerve to attend a service with Pat. He was so outgoing; we weren't. It was an unusual layout. The church service was held upstairs. As we approached the second floor, it was noticeably different than anything we were used to. Not that we were regular church attendees, but sometimes we would go to the Catholic church we were married in or my Memere's congregational church in Spencer. This church was open and very bright. There were no shrines, no stained glass, no incense, no holy water, no pews, no organ, and no choir. Patrick waved us to sit with him in the front. I would have preferred a spot near the rear or by an exit. I was wearing all white, a long white skirt and a white summer top. I must have stuck out like a large marshmallow. I really felt out of place. People were overtly friendly. Whenever the service began, I was as nervous as a long-tailed cat in a room full of rocking chairs. I wanted out. The music was so corny. And way too many people were happy, clapping and all. Herb and I looked at each other to plan an escape, but we didn't feel like that would be appropriate because we would be noticed since we were right up front. We felt more like hostages. Patrick fit right in with the congregation. The songs they were singing were not hymns. I never heard of this kind of music before. But we patiently stuck it through, and I'm so glad we did. It was the sermon that struck our hearts. It felt like everything this preacher was saying was directed specifically for us and the situation we were in. From that point on, we were hooked.

Here's a funny introduction! When Herb was setting the toilet in the downstairs bathroom at the church, he felt cornered by two older men who were members. Harold and Marvin were blocking his entrance. Marvin bluntly asked Herb if he knew God. Herb was taken back by his question. Herb admitted he knew God in a cautious manner. Marvin asked Herb if he knew who Jesus was. Herb replied, "No." Suddenly Marvin pulled a tract (a brochure or leaflet that churches supply or hand out to the public that gives information to visitors about God) out of his rear pocket and started pointing passionately to the booklet, explaining to Herb the only way to heaven and God the Father was through God's Son, Jesus. As much as Marvin was eager to share his faith with Herb, it was definitely an unusual and awkward approach.

Some of my friends have their loved ones' birthdays down to a science. Not me. But I will never forget December 12, 2006. It was the most profound, pivotal moment in my entire life. Herb and I were invited by Pastor Ron and his wife, Sherry, for lunch downtown at a pizza place. They made us feel welcome and comfortable; they had the gift of hospitality. They seemed kind and genuine. Pastor didn't waste much time; there was minimal small talk. He was a candid man and got right to the point. He asked me a question that I really didn't like to think about. He said, "Kristi, if you were to die tonight and meet God at the pearly gates in heaven, why should He let you in?" It felt like a trick question. I felt like I was put on the spot. I didn't know the answer. I told Pastor that He didn't have to let me in, that I hoped He would, but He's God; therefore, God doesn't have to do anything. Pastor made this loud buzzer sound, kind of like the annoying noise you hear on the game show *Jeopardy!* when a contestant declares the incorrect answer. He loudly said, "Wrong answer!" I could feel frustration rising up in me. I didn't want to be rude, especially to a pastor of a church, but I asked him point-blank, "What makes you think you're going to heaven and I'm not?" He smiled patiently and returned his answer to my question with these humble words: "I am just a beggar telling another beggar where to find bread."

He had my attention. I was curious and couldn't wait for him to reveal the answer to me. He proceeded to explain that Jesus is the answer. Jesus is the way to heaven. He is the Son of God. He came to earth to become the perfect sacrifice, to die on the cross for my sins and the sins of the world. His desire is for no one to perish or go to hell. We all have a choice to accept Jesus as our Lord and Savior. We have free will. God will not force us to love him. I have heard of Jesus before, and I have heard of God, but not like this! Pastor explained to me that God really loves *me*! When Pastor said those words to me, I heard truth for the first time. I believed him. I felt unconditional love like never before.

Maybe I was arrogant, but when he told me He died for my sins, I really thought to myself, *What sins?* Was I that ignorant to think that I wasn't a sinner? I told him that I was a good person and that my mom always taught me that God wouldn't send a good person to hell. Pastor Ron asked me to define "good." The most I knew of the Ten Commandments were, "Thou shalt not kill." I told the pastor that I never murdered anyone. He said, "Okay, but have you ever helped yourself to something that didn't belong to you?" I had to admit, yes. Even though I didn't consider myself a kleptomaniac, I took a couple packs of sticky notes from my old job once, and I dared my mother-in-law to steal a cheap pair of earrings with me from a department store. Pastor went on to explain how God's Son died to wipe away all the sins of mankind. Could I really be that blinded?

But Pastor Ron wasn't finished. While we were in our old jalopy waiting in their driveway, by this point, he extended an invitation to me and Herb. He asked me if I would like to welcome Jesus into my heart and receive the free gift of salvation. Would I like to *know* that I will go to heaven too? Usually, I had a difficult time accepting anything from others, especially if it was free (remember my pride?), but not then. I was ready. No sooner could I respond back with a yes that I got overwhelmingly emotional. I was sitting in the back seat weeping. It wasn't a pretty sight. Sherry was fumbling to find me a Kleenex. I was a sniffling snotty mess. I repeated the prayer after him with my whole heart and made the best decision of my life. I was washed clean and born from above or "born again," as they call it. I felt different right away. A huge burden lifted from my soul. I noticed I no longer had the fear of dying (which used to consume me). I felt *peace* for the first time.

Then it was Herb's turn; he also trusted in Jesus that day. Something miraculous happened. Herb told me the hole in his heart (from his father's death) was gone. The aching sensation he had for many years disappeared. It was a pinch-me moment.

Herb and I had a hunger to know more about God. We bought a New Living Translation Bible (for the easier reading level) and read through the whole thing in less than a year. That speaks volumes because I'm not by nature a book reader. I tried to read from the King James Version before, but I couldn't get past all the *thee*s and *thou*s. It was fascinating to finally connect pieces to a life puzzle of questions. It made sense when someone explained to me that the Bible was a love letter written to God's children. Your eyes will be open when you have the Holy Spirit dwelling inside you. The Holy Spirit (who is the Third Person of the Trinity) comes into your life when you ask Jesus to be your Lord and Savior.

I don't know about you, but have odd things happened to you after you had a brief thought or inkling about something? There were instances where I would have a thought or a dream about something in particular, and it would actually take place in real life. Little things like getting the feeling that I was going to be pulled over that day by a police officer, or just knowing that something was wrong with my twin, and she would call me right after. I remember my mom was the same way; she had instinctual knowledge about certain things. A common practice for me was to jot it down when I'd get a premonition.

Cleaning through some old papers, I came across one of these notes I managed to write on the back of a bookmark. The date was written in black ink. It was September 25, 2006. I remember that when I wrote this, I had a fear that I was about to die soon. It read:

> I'm not ready. I can hear Your whisper. Please come to me slowly. Yes, I'm afraid. I do believe in You. I've known You for a long time. Sometimes You allow yourself in quietly, and other times Your knock is loud. I hear You. I'm sorry if I pretend I can't. I want to know and love You, but I'm still afraid.

This intimate conversation was between me and God. I was flabbergasted when I read it. I had an awareness that there was significant legitimacy in my words. It was less than eighty days prior to the day I was born again! I did, in fact, die! Just not the way I expected. I died to myself. The old me was gone and buried. All my past sins were washed away as far as the east is from the west. I was a brand-new person. Second Corinthians 5:17 says, "Therefore, if anyone is in Christ, he is a new creation. The old has passed away; behold, the new has come." I really appreciate the way the English Standard Version says it. It also reminds me of Revelation 3:20: "Look! I stand at the door and knock. If you hear my voice and open the door, I will come in, and we will share a meal together as friends."

How many times have I heard the popular Christian hymn "Amazing Grace"? Almost every single time I listened to that song, I was deeply moved by it. I loved the melody, and the words were so touching. The fact that anyone would depict themselves as a wretch, how honest was that? Of course, the well-known line "I once was blind, but now I see"—see what? What exactly did that verse mean? Music was a personal way to reach the inner core of my soul. Many people have resorted to tears by the power of that song, me being one of them. I didn't know who "Grace" was, until now. If you are a believer and received Jesus into your life, then you can comprehend what I'm saying. If you haven't made that decision for yourself *yet*, then the only way I can describe it is like this: Recently, I went to the Cheesecake Factory with my girlfriends from high school. We were celebrating our birthdays together: August is Tina's, September is mine, October is Emma's, and January is Marsha's. By the way, the best flavored cheesecake is, by far, the pineapple upside-down cheesecake, just sayin'. I noticed, as we are in our forties now, that the topics of our conversations were changing drastically from when we were in our twenties. I boasted to the girls that I was so thankful I didn't need glasses. Three out of four of us were using them to order from our menus, me being the one who still had twenty-twenty vision. Marsha had an inexpensive purple-framed pair of reading glasses hanging around her neck. I asked her if she would mind if I tried them on. The strength was +1.25. I thought it would be amusing. The joke was on me!

How was it possible that I had gone through my days and not even know that I wasn't seeing at my full potential? I realized that if I'm reading something with fine print in order for me to focus, I have to adjust the object a little further from my face. But it was so subtle. I was amazed at how clearer the letters were on the bifold of that menu, and the lesson I learned was, our perception can change. Not that I was blind, but I understood the fact that sometimes we don't realize how obscure our vision really is. I didn't know I needed a Savior; I was blinded and unaware. I didn't know that, according to God, I was considered a sinner. But once I made that decision to follow Him, the words "I once was blind, but now I see" became real for me. I got the meaning to those words in a much clearer way than ever before.

Even though we were in the middle of a three-year lawsuit, the sting was beginning to subside. We were still suffering from the consequences of working for Herb's uncle, but now we had a ray of hope.

We felt comfortable confiding in Pastor Ron and his wife, Sherry, about the difficulties we were facing. It felt so reassuring to have their support. Life wasn't a bed of roses for them either. They might not have encountered our exact hardship, but they sure experienced times in the valley as well. They invested in us during a time we felt abandoned and criticized. They interceded for us and prayed often on our behalf. Finally, we had someone to lean on. At a time when we were paired with scandal, we recognized our relationships were deteriorating. Friends and family seemed to lose faith in us.

As we reflect on the circumstances of the way we came to receive Jesus into our lives, it is clear how patient God was with us. When we refer to our testimony, we warn others how stubborn we were. Often we begin the story by saying, "God slammed a baseball bat to our knee caps to get our attention." Unfortunately, it was the only way we would submit to His authority. He tried many times before in subtlety. We were full of arrogance and pride. I think one of the hardest things for a controlling person with trust issues like me was to surrender and trust in God. Some people have a very different experience when they convert to Christ. Some people do not require God's discipline or wrath. Some people don't have to experience hardships or loss to get the picture. They just willingly receive Jesus. But at the end of the day, as terrifying as the experience has been, I wouldn't change a thing. Everyone has their own story, and as difficult as it has been, it is ours.

What if you knew the location of an endless supply of gold, and you wanted to bless your loved ones, knowing full well you'd have more than enough treasure to reserve for yourself and future generations? Wouldn't you want to tell others? Would you offer to help them live a life of freedom, far from poverty and oppression? How many times have you told a friend about the clearance sale you found on an item? Have you flashed your lights to an oncoming stranger to warn them their speeding may get them a ticket by the police officer you just passed by who was parked about a quarter of a mile up the street? Most of us like to be the bearer of good news.

Do you know what the definition of Gospel is? The word *gospel* comes from the Old English *god*, meaning "good," and *spel*, meaning "news, a story." In Christianity, the term "good news" refers to the story of Jesus Christ's birth, death, and resurrection. Now that's *Good News*! With that being said, I know many people, including some of those that I love, claim their belief in Jesus to be a private matter. This is concerning to me and quite serious. In my opinion, the worst thing we can do to our fellow brothers and sisters is remain passive and mute. How can we just selfishly sit on heaps and piles of golden treasure? God says in 1 Chronicles 16:24, "Declare his glory among the nations, his marvelous deeds among the peoples." And in 1 Peter 3:15 NIV, it reads, "But in your hearts revere Christ as Lord. Always be prepared to give an answer to everyone who asks you to give the reason for the hope you have. But do this with gentleness and respect." When Herb and I accepted Jesus, we shouted from the rooftops! We thought everyone we knew would want to hear what we had to say. But not everyone was as thrilled to hear the good news as we were. Then I remembered when my sister tried to save me with holy water; I realized it's not my job to save anyone. My responsibility is to simply tell anyone who may be willing to listen. With that comes much prayer as well. I can't change anyone. The power doesn't come from me. Only God can open hearts. I'm living proof of that!

It is my pure pleasure to extend an invitation to you, to offer you the same hope that was extended to me over fourteen years ago. If you've never made Jesus your personal Lord and Savior, and you would like to know without a doubt that God will adopt you into His family and forgive you just like He has forgiven me, it's not a magic potion or fancy words. Confess with your mouth (preferably out loud if you are able) and repeat these words: Lord Jesus, I believe You are the only Son of God. Thank You for dying on the cross for me. I know I have sinned, and I am not perfect. Would You forgive me and make me new? I welcome the Holy Spirit to teach me your ways and open my eyes to your truth. I believe in my heart that God raised you from the dead, and You are seated in heaven next to the Father. Would You adopt me into your family? In Jesus Name I Pray. Amen!

If you just said that prayer with a sincere heart, welcome to the family! May God bless you on your journey and show you your purpose in Him! We are not meant to walk this life alone. Find a Bible-believing church and get plugged in. Don't be surprised when you open your Bible and you find the Lord revealing more of Himself to you. It's a relationship, not a religion.

If you simply aren't ready to commit yourself to Jesus. ask God to help you develop your faith and see what happens! "Everyone who calls on the name of the Lord will be saved" (Romans 10:13). Also know that I will be praying for anyone who reads this book to have a saving encounter with God Almighty. But know, the choice is ultimately yours. You have the freedom to choose Him or to reject Him; that's the beauty of free will.

Less than a couple weeks after I was saved, I landed in the emergency room. I was doubled over in excruciating pain and could barely walk. I insisted Herb take me to the hospital and told him he had no time to spare. My body was weak. I had heart palpitations and spasms. The pain was so severe. My sister came for support; she was always a comfort to me. I pleaded with Herb to go through red lights if he had to. Every bump from the road was torment. My sister and Herb assisted me to the emergency room, and when I lifted my head, I was in deep despair. The room was chock-full of patients waiting to be seen. There was no way I felt I could make it for hours in this agony. I felt bad for one person I saw in a wheelchair. The wound on their foot was oozing, and they didn't have a choice but to sit there and wait. Lord, have mercy!

As we were registering, I could see my sister was anxious. I was trying to hold it together for her sake, but I really had no idea what was wrong with me. The nurse didn't seem to have much compassion. I was treated like a number, not like a human being. That's fine when you're in line at the deli in a grocery store, but not in a hospital, for crying out loud! She said there was a bug going around and assured me that I would be fine. My sister persisted to tell the nurse that I didn't have a "bug," that she believed something more serious was occurring. My sister confessed to me she wanted to punch that woman in the face for being so obstinate.

I wouldn't call myself OCD; however, I do like my surroundings to be clean. I asked Keri to take me to the bathroom next to the waiting room. She brought me in, and I began crying. The bathroom was gross, and there was no privacy. But I didn't care. I was on the floor; nothing mattered at this point. I told her to pray over me and read me my last rites. (She was a nun. I heard when a person is on their deathbed, they can receive a final prayer before they pass on to the next life). I was so disappointed. I can remember thinking, *I'm only twelve days saved, and I have no treasures stored up in heaven.* Even though I was thankful to know I would go to heaven, I felt so incomplete. I never got to fulfill the dream of being a momma. I had so much to offer still, and I felt like it was being cut short. I had no control.

As Keri began praying, I heard a faint voice calling out in the waiting room, "Crystal Seymour? Is there a Crystal Seymour?" I was so relieved! I told Keri to wheel me out of the bathroom quickly so we wouldn't lose our place. A nurse helped me into a bed. They ran tests, and they diagnosed me with hypokalemia (which is low potassium). My levels were dangerously low. I felt brand-new when they stuck my arm with the much-needed fluids, and the pain finally subsided. What an answer to prayer! The doctor said it's a common misdiagnosis in emergency rooms and can be life-threatening.

What I learned that day is how unexpectedly we can leave this world, and we are absolutely powerless. When it's our time to go, we better be ready. I was thankful that I would have known the right answer if I met God at the pearly gates that day. If God asked me why He should let me in, I would have happily answered that I belonged to Jesus!

Speak Life

The tongue is a small thing that makes grand speeches. But a tiny spark can set a great forest on fire. And among all the parts of the body, the tongue is a flame of fire. It is a whole world of wickedness, corrupting your entire body. It can set your whole life on fire, for it is set on fire by hell itself.

—James 3:3–6 NLT

People thought we went off the deep end. They noticed we were changing. One of the first noticeable behaviors was our habit of swearing was decreasing significantly. Remember Patrick losing his bad habit of swearing? It wasn't uncommon for me to cuss. I reluctantly admit I found a foul mouth to be liberating. I could express myself without limits and add some shock value to get my point across. I admit, I could curse worse than a truck driver. Don't ask me why truck drivers have a reputation of vulgarity, but I was no better. That was one instant bad habit that we were convicted of. We heard of a swear jar being a helpful way for us to repel from blurting out obscene language. It was a visual reminder that helped discourage us from a loose tongue. Each time we caught ourselves saying a foul word, it cost us a quarter. It didn't take us long to fill up the container.

Words have power, the power to plant a seed of hope or to pull something apart in pieces. A compliment can build someone up, but a critical word can bring shame and even make someone feel self-conscious for years. God's Word says in Matthew 12:34–37 NLT, "You brood of snakes! How could evil men like you speak what is good and right? For whatever is in your heart determines what you say. A good person produces good things from the treasury of a good heart, and an evil person produces evil things from the treasury of an evil heart. And I tell you this, you must give an account on judgement day for every idle word you speak. The words you say will either acquit you or condemn you." Ouch! I would have to admit, I'm at fault for many words over my lifetime that haven't been from a good heart, both from when I was an unbeliever and since being a follower of Jesus.

I can remember early in my walk with God, He would lovingly discipline me and nudge my heart to make things right with others I have hurt. One instance, I told God I would if I could, but I had no way to reach the person He laid on my heart. He responded. *Did you forget Facebook?* Wow, I can't believe He is asking me to contact this person on Facebook and risk being rejected or, worse, offended. What if she attacks me back? What if this person has no idea what I am apologizing for? What if I'm waking a sleeping giant? After mustering up the courage, I went on Facebook and sought out this person I spoke very harshly to many years ago. I was surprised that she even accepted my friend request! Then I private-messaged her straight from my heart with a sincere apology. After I said I was sorry for the words I said to her the last time we spoke, I asked her if she even remembered what I was referring to. My heart hurt when she replied yes. Wow, she's been living with these words of condemnation for so long, and with my weaponized mouth, I was the one who aimed and fired those horrible words. She kindly accepted my apology, and the gift was all mine. I felt so thankful for her grace and her mercy toward me. The very next day, I had a sense I was going to bump into her, and guess what, I did! I was on a dinner date with my honey, and there she was, over to my right with her parents. I approached her and gave her and her family a hug and expressed my gratitude for her forgiveness. Another "wow God" moment for me.

Herb began a new routine of carrying a piece of coal in his pocket. This also helped him remember the consequences of his words. I'm sure it ended up in the washing machine a few times, but it was effective. He was inspired by Isaiah 6:6–7 NLT: "Then one of the seraphim [an angelic being] flew to me with a burning coal he had taken from the altar with a pair of tongs. He touched my lips with it and said, 'See this coal has touched your lips. Now your guilt is removed, and your sins are forgiven.'"

Being a single mom of three kids must have brought great fear over my mom as Keri and I began to develop into womanhood. Being pregnant with one child was difficult, but being surprised with twins toward the end of her first pregnancy must have brought on many emotions. Sure, hearing someone is having twins is special, but from the perspective of a teenage mother without a husband or financial support justifiably can cause some doubts, I would assume. Let's just say I witnessed my mom do things the hard way. I knew early on I didn't want to follow her footsteps. I'm pretty sure my mom didn't want us girls going through the difficulties she went through while she uttered the words of disapproval to us at a young age. She used to bluntly (with no filter) say things like, "You better not get pregnant!" "You better not get knocked up!" It's not like Keri and I were promiscuous, but sometimes I did get resentful when she would assume I was sexually active when clearly I was not. It did put a fear in me early on. I barely understood the birds and the bees. It's not like we talked a lot about that subject, and if we did, I felt a lot of shame and negativity. I wasn't comfortable talking about those things at all. I was a modest girl.

Keep in mind, my mom was not a believer the time she said those things to me. It took me some time, but with God's help, I was able to forgive her. Parents may not realize it or not, but they have spiritual authority over their children. I'm not placing blame directly on my mom for not being able to conceive a child, but was it possible that her words did damage? According to the Word, yes. "The tongue can bring death or life; those who love to talk reap the consequences" (Proverbs 18:21).

I realized, now that I was under the authority of Jesus, I needed to rebuke the words that were spoken over me as a child to break free from any curses, known or unknown, and claim that I will receive the promises God has for me. At this point, we were about six years into unexplainable infertility. I had already undergone a laparoscopic procedure that confirmed my hunch that I had endometriosis. My twin sister, Keri, already had the same procedure and recommended

I get checked too to see if I had the same physical issues that she was diagnosed with. Even after the four-hour surgery in Foxboro, I wasn't healed. I hoped the doctors would remove it all and I would be able to conceive again.

Herb told me when his dad used to get really angry, he would bite his tongue and yell, "You're gonna be the death of me!" So you can imagine how hard that would be for Herb and his brothers when their father died at the young age of thirty-nine. Words can leave a damaging and lasting imprint on our souls.

Most of us have suffered from some form of abuse in our lives. It could be a boyfriend, a girlfriend, a spouse, a grandparent, a minister, a teacher, a coach, people in authority, a boss, a coworker, a parent, a bully, a teenager, or even a child! Not that pain can be measured, but without a doubt, verbal abuse is not any less painful than being abused physically. Maybe it's easier to comprehend when someone is being slapped, pushed, choked, or intimidated with a weapon that this form of abuse is much more severe. That's not always the case. It's so important not to minimize or compare someone else's suffering. Verbal abuse can cause extensive damage. Being called names or being put down, someone screaming at you, intentionally embarrassing you, controlling you, accusing you, manipulating you, or threatening you is all about power and can chip away at your self-worth. Even when you are removed from the perpetrator, these abusive words that have been absorbed into your mind can cause lasting hurt and trauma. Evil words can leave invisible scars. The scars may not be noticeable to the naked eye, but words do have the power to echo years of emotional suffering.

If words didn't hold the power of life and death, then how is it that a suicidal person can be prevented to carry out the act of ending their life when someone persuades that person through mere words not to end their lives? The convincing tone of someone who really cares can make a difference. My husband can attest to this firsthand. For reasons of anonymity, let's just call the man Gary. A guy named Gary reached out to Herb and texted him clearly stating he was ready to end his life. He was thanking Herb for his friendship and feeling unworthy of being loved because he felt condemnation for his past sins. As he was expressing his goodbyes, he seemed to lose all hope for his future, and according to his state of mind, there was no sense in going on. Herb took him very seriously even though he only knew him for a short time. He offered him a place to rest for the night and interceded in prayer for him with deep anguish and concern. Herb purposely kept him texting continuously in an effort to keep him focused on the moment, drawing him into conversation to distract him. We immediately called out for prayer on his behalf with sensitivity to his privacy. We were burdened by the seriousness of the threat. Thank God he didn't go through with his intentions. We believe God intervened, and his life was spared.

What about the importance of declaring our sacred wedding vows? When someone promises God as their witness for better or for worse, for richer or poorer, in sickness and in health, to love and to cherish, till death do they part—what is the binding force? Is it the rings? The witnesses? Or is it the actual words they speak that seal the deal?

I came across the strangest experiment on You Tube. Not that everything you see on the internet is factual. It's a recreation of Dr. Masaru Emoto's rice experiment. You put cooked rice into three separate glass containers. You label the first one "I love you," the second "I hate you," and the third you leave blank. Every day you send affectionate thoughts and repeat kind words of love and emphasize positive words to the jar that is labeled "I love you." Then you would also send bad, negative energy and words to the second jar that is labeled "I hate you." The third jar you disregard completely. By the end of thirty days, you can see the jar of rice labeled "I love you" is still pure white and looks virtually the same as day one. The jar of rice that is labeled "I hate you" is full of mold. And the third jar was the worst of all, with black mold growing all over the rice that was once as white as the "I love you" jar. I don't doubt the results of this experiment. It's a great reminder to speak life and acknowledge others instead of assuming they know you love or care about them.

There are studies that prove talking to your plants does, in fact, help them grow. So if that's the case, then we have an opportunity every minute of every day to make a huge difference. Our words can have a ripple effect for generations.

Stay away from gossip, mockery, slander, and bearing false witness. One great way to check if what you're saying is okay is to imagine if the person you are speaking about was sitting in the room and could hear your conversation. Would they be hurt by your words? Would you want someone else saying those exact same words about you?

A prayer is basically words, a conversation between you and God. Prayer by definition is a solemn request for help or expression of thanks addressed to God. Make no mistake, there is power in your prayers!

In the beginning was the Word, and the Word was with God, and the Word was God (John 1:1). Jesus is often referred to as the "Word made flesh." So the Word became human and made His home among us. He was full of unfailing love and faithfulness. And we have seen His glory, the glory of the Father's one and only Son (John 1:14 NLT). When we read the Bible, the Word is alive! Many of God's children can read one verse in the Bible and receive truth from God in multiple ways. He reaches us in a personal, intimate way when we spend time in His Word. It is one of the many ways He connects with us.

In the beginning, God spoke everything into existence. That blows my mind! And *God said*, "Let there be light," and there was light. And *God said*, "Let there be a vault between the waters to separate water from water" (Genesis 1:3). And *God said*, "Let the water under the sky be gathered to one place, and let the ground appear" (Genesis 1:6). And it was so. And *God said*, "Let the land produce vegetation: seed-bearing plants and trees on the land that bear fruit with seed in it, according to their various kinds" (Genesis 1:9), and it was so. And *God said*, "Let there be lights in the vault of the sky to separate the day from night, and let them serve as signs to mark sacred times, and days, and years, and let them be lights in the vault of the sky to give light on the earth" (Genesis 1:11), and it was so. And *God said*, "Let the land produce living creatures according to their kinds: the livestock, the creatures that move along the ground, and the wild animals, each according to its kind," and it was so. Then *God said*, "Let us make mankind in our image, in our likeness, so that they may rule over the fish in the sea and the birds in the sky, over the livestock and all the wild animals, and over all the creatures that move along the ground" (Genesis 1:24). You get the point? And it was so. It is such a mystery! But if we are created in the image of God and He creates through speaking words out of His mouth, then is it possible to say that our words have power too? How thought-provoking!

Let's try not to fall into habitual words that cause harm to ourselves or others. I hate when I hear people call themselves an idiot, stupid, or some other comment that puts themselves down. Maybe positive words don't roll off your tongue easily. Maybe it feels awkward to say something kind because you're afraid it will not sound authentic. Let me challenge you to do it anyway! If you don't have a gift for words of affirmation, practice daily until it becomes more natural.

Maybe you'd find it easier to write it down in a card or a letter. A scrap piece of paper, a Post-it note, or even lipstick on a mirror works too! I encourage you to initiate and practice repetition. We can reteach and reprogram ourselves! The absence of words like "I love you," "I'm proud of you," "I believe in you," and "I'm thankful for you" can cause spiritual suffering. Rejection and neglect can cause serious symptoms of depression. Who doesn't want to feel accepted, loved, valued, and significant?

Ever since I learned there is power in words, I plaster scripture throughout my home. One that I love is written in chalk on a small chalkboard from 1 Samuel 25:6: "Long life to you! Good health to you and your household! And good health to all that is yours!" I declare these things over myself and my loved ones. I love signage too. I find random signs from yard sales and flea markets that cause me to pause and think. Here are just a few: "Families are forever," "We may not have it all together, but together we have it all," "Blessed and grateful," "Never get so busy making a living that you forget to make a life," "It is well with my soul," "There is always something to be thankful for," "If light is in your heart, you will find the way home." And one of my favorites: "Love truthfully."

I'm pretty sure I'll have my fair share of coal when I meet the Lord, but I do make an effort to choose my words wisely, and I'm always asking God to help me tame this tongue! When was the last time someone said they loved you? When was the last time you told someone you loved them?

Answered Prayer

I waited patiently for the Lord to help me, and he turned to me and heard my cry. He lifted me out of the pit of despair, out of the mud and the mire. He set my feet on solid ground and steadied me as I walked along. He has given me a new song to sing, a hymn of praise to our God. Many will see what he has done and be amazed. They will put their trust in the Lord. Oh, the joys of those who trust the Lord, who have no confidence in the proud or in those who worship idols. O Lord my God, you have performed many wonders for us. Your plans for us are too numerous to list. You have no equal. If I tried to recite all your wonderful deeds, I would never come to the end of them.

—Psalm 40:1–5 NLT

Fifteen years is a long time to suffer from the debilitating effects of endometriosis (an incurable chronic disorder when tissue that lines the uterus grows outside the uterus and can be found on the ovaries, fallopian tubes, or the intestines). Month after month, I was miserable, finding no relief from the excruciating pain of heavy periods. All I wanted was to just lie on the cold floor in the fetal position with a bottle of ibuprofen. Even after the four-hour surgery to remove the endometriosis, I wasn't healed. We went through months of fertility treatments. The expense was costly on our pocketbooks, our time, and my health. You can't be on Clomid for more than a few months at a time. The drug causes superovulation, producing more than one egg each cycle to give higher odds of pregnancy. It isn't uncommon for twins or multiple pregnancies to occur when this treatment is being administered. I was so desperate to get pregnant I even agreed to inject myself with the hormone human chorionic gonadotrophin (hcG).

We were traveling to doctors all over the state of Massachusetts getting nowhere, and the months that passed by turned into years. I would cry a lot and wonder why I still had faith for a family of our own. I struggled trying to convince my honey that I believed we would have a baby. High highs and low lows. It felt like a roller coaster of insanity. We were aggressively trying to fix our problem. The clock was ticking, and the pressure caused an insurmountable amount of stress. I can see why many couples don't make it through the challenges of infertility. We reduced our standards in ways that eventually led to frustration and resentment. It's humiliating and humbling to go to these doctors and get open and personal about a topic that is so private.

It was around this time I left my position at the bank. I was there for roughly seven years, and I knew If I wanted to focus on getting my health in order and eventually starting a family, I needed to lower my expectations for myself and leave my job. Even though they were really understanding and supportive, I was losing a lot of work while trying to schedule all of my doctor's appointments.

It takes me a while to process my thoughts and to comprehend some things. Whether it's a few minutes or a couple weeks, I can get a lightbulb moment past the expiration date of a joke. Usually Herb can tell when I have this delay because of the confused blank stare on my face. He will ask me after the punch line, "Do you get it?" Sometimes he would smile and laugh at my expense when I would reluctantly admit that I didn't understand. And when I ask him to repeat it to me, he just shakes his head and rolls his eyes at me.

I'm pretty sure that was God's expression when it literally took me three months to figure out—I was healed of endometriosis! I can date it back to the day I surrendered my heart to Jesus. I noticed when I was due for my "friend" (more like my enemy) that I was not in any pain at all. I remember thinking, *I'm not going to get away with this. Next month, it will probably be really severe.* Then the second month came, no pain. Still I didn't relate the absence of pain to any explanation. It was the third month when I had an epiphany. *You've got to be kidding me! Jesus healed me!* I was jumping for joy and so elated! You might have thought I just won the lottery! I was almost embarrassed it took me three solid months to figure out I was healed. No one can convince me otherwise. The experience I had belonged to me. It was a gift. I just *knew* that I knew I was healed 100 percent. I knew I was finally free from the repetitive pain I suffered from every month. I learned my God was not only my Savior; He was my Healer. Joy doesn't even describe the emotion I had when I recognized the gift He gave me. The other thing I found difficult was due to its personal nature, it's not like I could go tell everyone openly about my healing. I shared the awesome news with close relatives and friends.

A group of women from my church and I went to Mount Monadnock for a weekend retreat. I freely worshiped that weekend and put a folded up piece of paper inside the box of prayer requests. It was a written prayer that asked Jesus to bless me and my honey with a child.

We contemplated fostering children or adoption, but I was dead set against it for many years because of the difficulty we experienced seeing what foster children can suffer. The system seemed to fail the children, and I had a fear that if we fell in love with a child, the biological parents would change their minds and take their child, along with our hearts, away from us. The risk was so grueling. But something shifted and changed our minds. I felt like there were so many children who needed love and a good home, and we were eager and willing. We had this huge empty house, and our hearts were open. At that point, I didn't care whose child it was; I just wanted to be a momma, and I knew my honey would make a great dad. So we took the steps to apply for a MAPP (Massachusetts Department of Children and Families) training course and summoned up the courage that one way or another, we were going to be parents. Even though there are no guarantees, we were hoping we would be united with a sibling group (we hated the idea of siblings being separated).

During this same time, we were seeking financial counseling from our church. They were offering help for people that wanted to learn how to be good stewards of what God gave them and how to become better disciplined with our finances in hopes to become free and simplify. We were working diligently to preserve our credit and protect everything that we worked so hard for. Harold Harper agreed to meet with us periodically and teach us the basics from materials of Crown Financial Ministries. We learned how to budget, what a tithe was, and he would share some of his failures from his past and how he and his wife Jane were able to become financially free by learning basic principles and applying them steadily over the years. We needed guidance especially in the area of finances, we learned the wrong way. We were up to our ears in debt from our teens, we were tired of the rat race and we were eager to find relief.

Harold understood most of the financial hardship was pressing us due to the lawsuit. It clouded us with great oppression and was causing intense stress. He made sure we were accountable and signed an agreement that promised we will do our best to follow the plan (for our own good). He didn't mind investing in us but wanted to make sure we weren't wasting his time or ours. The following meeting when we met up with Harold, he leaned over to me and told me he didn't know how I'd been able to juggle the debt and bills the way we'd been doing for so long. He said he had to put away the numbers because he was getting a headache! Finally, someone understood the stress I was under. I felt validated. He also spoke life to me that day. He said, "Kristi, when you get your finances in order, you will be able to get pregnant." The way he said those words to me were so matter-of-fact. I cherished those words and held on to them tightly with a newfound hope and a countenance of joy.

After several weeks of MAPP classes, we felt hope-filled that finally another lifelong dream was going to happen. We waited ten years to get our dream home, and it was about nine years by this point of trying for a family. There are some rare cases that foster parents could have a placement with basically no notice. Some foster parents have had spontaneous and unexpected phone calls that informed them they could pick up their newborn baby in days or even hours! It was exhilarating to think we could have an instant family.

We began preparing by painting the rooms upstairs and furnishing them with gender neutral decorations. We had two twin beds with comforters and a bureau. Across the hall in the other bedroom, we set up a white wooden baby crib. I bought a small mint-green pillow with ruffles that had the word "Believe" embroidered and placed it inside the crib. We were so nervous and excited. Then it occurred to me. A fleeting thought came and went. I felt like we had one last shot at trying to conceive a child of our own. I asked my honey if he would consider one final time trying fertility treatment. I shared with him that I was willing. We knew it was frowned upon by the MAPP class. I expressed to my honey that I know we tried for years on our own, but my thought was, why don't we give it one more last effort now that we have Jesus!

I was so glad Herb agreed, but he made it clear that we were only going for it one last time. We didn't want to jeopardize the opportunity to adopt, so we didn't verbalize our intentions to the social worker. The appointment was made with the specialist at the Reproductive Science Center in Lexington, and I began one round of hormones. We wanted to be aggressive, and we were suggested another IUI (intrauterine insemination). We questioned what was acceptable to God. Did God approve of doctors getting involved with the process of fertility? When was it considered pushing the envelope in God's eyes? There is human manipulation in the process, which means the chance of human error too. Were we doing something immoral? The bottom line is, we realized God is fully in control. If He didn't want this to happen, it's not going to. God reads our hearts. We're not claiming to be God or "play" God. It very much still requires great faith to go forward with fertility procedures. We were comfortable making the decision to go ahead. God gave us peace on the matter. We were fully submitted to God's will either way. We were ready to be parents either by conception or adoption. Faith without action is useless. We were flexing our spiritual muscles. The moment we got there, I had peace. Herb and I said a prayer in the room while we were waiting for the doctor to arrive. I assumed my doctor was going to be a male when I was told the name. A woman wearing a white lab coat, dark hair, a flawless complexion, and piercing blue eyes entered our room. Maybe you think I'm crazy, but I did wonder if she was an angelic being. She completed the procedure. The goal of an IUI is to increase the chance of fertilization. Women have a 10 to 20 percent chance of getting pregnant with just one IUI cycle. The more cycles you undergo, the higher the chance of pregnancy. We had one shot (pun intended) left. Herb appreciated her final suggestion. She advised us to go home and get intimate (if you know what I mean), so if I did, in fact, become pregnant, we wouldn't know if conception took place from the actual procedure or not. Herb was happy to oblige.

We completed our MAPP classes, and we were officially certified! Now all we had to do was wait and see if we would receive a call from the office. In the meantime, there were some signs that I might want to buy another pregnancy test. I can't tell you how many boxes I bought over the years! It was October 14, 2008, at 1:50 p.m. that I discovered two lines on the test stick that confirmed my hopes and dreams—we were finally *pregnant*! I waited almost three long hours (impatiently, I might add) for Herb to come home. I was bursting with joy. I wanted to announce the amazing news in person so I could witness his expression!

Endorphins kicked into overdrive! It was a high I can't explain. Even though negative thoughts tried to creep into my mind and plant seeds of doubt and fear, I was not tolerating them for one minute! I focused on enjoying every moment of this pregnancy, and I ignored anything that tried to trample on my joy. I was determined that this was our time. Then an interesting thing happened. When we opened an unfamiliar letter in the mail, we were shocked when it read, "Congratulations, your three children are approved for health care." I was confused by the letter, and Herb called to find out we were chosen for the placement of three sibling girls! I was so overwhelmed. I thought, *All I have ever wanted is to become a mom, and now in one year's time, I'm going to have four kids!* We called the social worker and explained we were pregnant. She was happy for us and told me that there is usually one couple in her class that ends up pregnant. She congratulated us and told us that she would find someone else to care for the girls. It was bittersweet. A part of me wanted them, but another part of me was relieved. She told us she would keep our file, and if we decided to pursue foster care or adoption, she would be happy to help us in the future.

Brushing my teeth made me gag. I was so nauseous. The smell of certain foods grossed me out. I chomped on a lot of ice cubes (something I rarely did before). Without a doubt, I was feeling the effects of morning sickness. I automatically assumed for some reason I'd be a beautiful petite pregnant woman with this cute little baby-bump belly. God had a sense of humor! I gained sixty pounds. Being five feet short and close to 190 pounds was not as adorable as I expected. I had a newfound sense of sympathy for obese people. I couldn't do a lot of the basics. Reaching every crevice for proper hygiene required physical skill just like playing the popular board game of Twister. I had to buy shoes that I could slip on because I couldn't even reach my feet to tie my shoes. I breathed heavier, and by the end of my pregnancy, I couldn't sleep because no matter how many pillows I had, I couldn't find a comfortable position. I felt guilty if I complained because I wanted this! What goes around comes around, honey. Payback was funny because now I was the one snoring!

Recognizing one of your family members on television could bring about feelings of, "Hey, I know that guy!" Or with pride, you can confidently say, "That man right there is related to me!" The shock of seeing Herb's uncle on the local news station claiming his fifteen seconds of fame fleeing to Venezuela on a private plane with his wife, five children, and the family dog with $1.3 million in stolen cash devastated us. The man on the TV screen couldn't be the same man we knew as family. It's difficult not to go into denial. There was a laundry list of charges against him. The last thing you want to admit to people is that he is of relation. He instantly brought shame to the family name—and we were bearing the same last name that we once used to claim with honor. We didn't want to be identified as a Seymour after this disgrace. A name we used to be so proud of was now stained.

Herb was working for a large outfit in Worcester. He sold his company to them and took on a three-year contract signing a no-compete clause. To be honest, I appreciated the steady weekly paychecks. In some ways, at first it was a huge relief; but in other ways, I know my honey felt like a caged bird. When the publicity came out about his uncle on the news and in the newspapers, it caused great stress for him. I remember Herb admitting that in an effort to protect his reputation and his position at the company, he felt compelled to scan any newspapers from the break room and remove any content that his uncle was featured in. He had so much fear and paranoia that he would be linked to his uncle at his job that any time his boss mentioned he wanted to have a talk, Herb would sweat bullets. Finally, he just couldn't take the torment any longer and asked to speak privately to his boss and to lay it all out on the table, knowing full well that he potentially could lose his career. That day when he came home, he was so relieved and free. His boss confided in Herb and reassured him that he had been through something similar in his past and not to worry.

The lawsuit was finally tapering off after many months; we were just waiting for a date from the courts. This was the third time I ever went to a trial. The first time, I was chosen for jury duty; the second time (a handful of years prior), I supported my twin sister when she testified that she was sexually assaulted by a priest; and this being the third time, I was there to back my husband (while I was very much pregnant) during this civil lawsuit. It was a foreign and intimidating experience. There was no support for my husband. I was it and, of course, his attorney, Dan. There were eight counts against him. The atmosphere was so intense. You know I was a prayer warrior that day! At one point, I excused myself to the ladies' room and just begged God to have mercy on my honey. I asked Him to be his advocate, to equip Herb with fortitude and give Dan the ability to defend my honey with boldness and wisdom. When Herb was called to the stand, I could tell he was nervous. He was out of his element. Even though Dan tried to prepare him, you could tell he was a fish out of water. This was unfamiliar territory. Herb didn't pull any punches, and he answered every question with honesty, even if it could be construed against him. He had nothing to hide. You could tell Dan was aggravated with Herb because he was giving more information than necessary. I was so thankful when the plaintiff was called to the stand because he was caught lying a few times. His testimony wasn't jiving with his paperwork, and he was avoiding answering the questions from Herb's attorney. After several attempts of asking the same question in different form, Dan yelled and said, "Judge, make him answer the question!" Then finally the judge heard enough. Talk about an answer to prayer: the judge cut off everyone and basically concluded with his decision. I listened as the wooden gavel slammed intermittently eight times between the words "NOT GUILTY" of each count against him. I knew God was present and how miraculous this was. The judge explained how obvious it was that Herb was duped by his uncle and taken advantage of and that it was clear Herb's uncle was the mastermind behind all these mortgage schemes. Again tears of gratitude and relief streamed down my cheeks. We celebrated by taking Dan out for lunch. After a few choice words, he said in all his years of practice, he has *never* witnessed a judge make a final decision verbally on the spot like that. Usually it comes weeks later in written form. We knew we were saved again by the grace of God.

Even though the experience of the lawsuits caused a lot of fear, trauma, and some gray hairs, it's for that very reason we hit rock bottom and learned how faithful God was and how to trust Him. The consequences of poor choices would eventually cost us more than we bargained for.

Our invitations for the baby shower read, "Baby girl or baby boy? Either one will bring much joy!" I printed them from my home computer featuring a background picture of the inside of the white crib that was upstairs in our home from when we were preparing to adopt a child. There was a whole new significance in the "Believe" pillow that was placed there months ago. We hosted our own couple's baby shower and felt it was most fitting to have the large event held at our church. We knew even the most non-churchgoing friends wouldn't miss our gathering. That was one way to get them to come to church! We must have had (without exaggeration) over one hundred people join us that day. It was a lot of fun. We had entertaining activities and competitions. One hilarious contest was who could drink apple juice out of a baby bottle the fastest (which, by the way, is a lot more difficult than it seems). A good friend from our church captured beautiful photographs of intimate pictures of me and Herb. One of my favorites was the humorous one where we are standing together facing each other, belly to belly, comparing whose tummy is bigger. Herb gained quite a bit of weight during my pregnancy.

Did you know almost half of expectant dads can gain up to thirty pounds during their partner's pregnancy? Some not only gain sympathy weight but claim to have symptoms like food cravings, nausea, anxiety, fatigue, odor aversions, and sleeping difficulties. Maybe my honey intentionally put on a "few" extra pounds (fifteen, to be exact) to help me feel better about myself. There was a scrapbook that I displayed with pictures of the ultrasounds and personal scriptures that were relevant for the occasion.

I appreciate this well-known scripture from Psalm 139:13–17 NLT:

> You made all the delicate, inner parts of my body and knit me together in my mothers' womb. Thank you for making me so wonderfully complex! Your workmanship is marvelous-how well I know it. You watched me as I was being formed in utter seclusion, as I was woven together in the dark of the womb. You saw me before I was born. Every day of my life was recorded in your book. Every moment was laid out before a single day had passed. How precious are your thoughts about me, O God. They cannot be numbered!

People were encouraged to write their thoughts and well wishes to the baby on pastel scraps of paper throughout the book. Herb and I both agreed that since we waited almost a decade for a baby, we could wait nine months to find out the gender of the child. I was so delighted we chose to keep it a mystery. The anticipation was a tease. We were beyond blessed. The baby didn't need anything. Everyone was so generous supplying our family with the latest baby supplies from a Diaper Genie, handmade quilts, bassinet, bibs, books, onesies, diapers, high chair, to babysitting coupons. Most baby items were either yellow or green, no pink or blues, and that was fine by me.

We might as well have thrown our childbirth classes right out the window. It was June 19, 2009, twenty minutes before midnight, that Herbert Francis Seymour IV was brought into this world. When the doctors announced he was a boy, he peed on me. Everyone got such a good laugh. I had to have a cesarean section. After many hours of labor and contractions, our baby was not descending. Maybe because he was a whopping ten pounds, three ounces, twenty-one inches long! I couldn't believe my eyes when I got to see him for the first time. I'm not gonna lie; my first reaction was to hope for some obvious "proof" that he was a product of his father. When I managed to peek over the blue cloth draped over me, I immediately noticed his dad's chiseled chin! I was overwhelmed with love! He was *perfect*! His facial features resembled an Eskimo. He had chubby cheeks, dark pigmented skin, fine dark-brown hair, and this perfect little nose. He definitely didn't get his nose from me! The experience of having a baby lacks words. It's probably the closest spiritual experience you can have being on this side of heaven. There was an instinctual surrender. I melted. I witnessed the miracle of life that day for the first time. It was indescribable. God's timing couldn't have been more precise. Little Herbie was born two days before Father's Day. It just doesn't get any better than that! All the sorrow, heartache, pain, and grief that used to darken that day was brought to light and joy and celebration! Gratitude for the experience of victory gave a top-of-the-mountain feeling.

We stayed at the hospital for five days. Many visitors came to see our newborn. My mom became a grammy again. This would be her fourth grandson, and Herb's mom and my uncle Mark were already assigned the title as "Mimi" and "Puppa" from our niece Kaydence. Mimi and Puppa were on a roll of being grandparents for the fourth time as well. Misty and Ray popped in and held the baby. You could see the love in their faces as they peeked down at this not-so-tiny miracle. We were excited to reciprocate the honor and asked them if they would be Little Herbie's godparents. It was so special that we were their oldest sons' godparents; now they would be ours.

One of the funniest first-time parent moments was when we needed to stop quickly at Walmart on the way home from the hospital. Picture two newbies looking at each other wondering who dealt it. Baby needed a diaper change, so we flipped up the hatchback door to our Rav4 and laid Little Herbie down. How difficult could this be? We assisted each other like it was a small surgical procedure. I was literally crying from laughing so hard. You could tell we had no finesse. Baby was squirming and making quite the mess. Number two was getting all over the place, and we must have used a whole package of baby wipes for one session. I'm telling you right now if Walmart parking lot had cameras on us, we could have made a lot of money on *America's Funniest Home Videos*!

When we came home, we were blessed with home-cooked meals for three weeks from family, friends, and church family! It was important to me that I was able to breastfeed the baby. What should just come naturally proved to be frustrating for both me and the baby. It was worse pain than the surgery! But I insisted and decided I was going to give my baby milk even if I had to pump. Being a first-time mom was scary. I remember the first couple days he was home. I put little hand mittens on him so he wouldn't scratch his face. He cried a lot and seemed to be very difficult to console. When I decided to give him a sponge bath, I was horrified to see his little finger was red and swollen. I noticed a piece of my hair managed to wrap around his finger. I immediately panicked and called the pediatrician. She warned me that is a common complaint with newborns. She tried to comfort me by saying they keep Nair (a lotion that removes hair) on hand for this very reason. Also, she said it could be worse for boys (I'll leave you to figure that out). Dad had pretty good eyesight and was able to locate the end of the piece of hair and gently unraveled it with tweezers from my son's tiny digit. From that point on, I realized this momma thing isn't gonna be easy.

Calgon, Take Me Away!

"For I know the plans I have for you," says the Lord." They are plans
for good and not for disaster, to give you a future and a hope."

—Jeremiah 29:11 NLT

Do you remember that commercial back in the 1980s of a woman soaking her cares away in a luxurious bubble bath trying to escape the day's stresses? I think if most moms were honest, we can relate to that commercial sometimes. Whoever said babies sleep a lot lied! I think God might have been a bit unfair at leaving the nursing up to just one parent. I did my best to keep up with everything, but I soon found myself feeling inadequate. I tried to adjust my expectations on myself and others, especially my honey. Sleep deprivation can cause insanity! Every two hours, Little Herbie was hungry. I felt like I gave birth to a toddler. He wanted meat and potatoes, and all I could offer was milk. I was a pumping machine! Taking a shower was a treat. I didn't feel comfortable with him out of my sight. Date nights were few and far between.

Thank God for the pacifier. I stood corrected to all the preconceptions of parental errors I swore I would never do. My mind set was apologetic to the moms before me. Now I understood from experience that it was wrong to judge other moms that resorted to bribery for one minute of peace. You have to remember, I was with my honey for eighteen years; now I had to share my husband, and my husband had to learn my attention was being demanded from a cute little brown-eyed monkey. This new life took a lot of sacrifice. It showed me just how selfish I was. Being a momma sucked every ounce of energy I had. I became a coffee drinker in need of the added boost from caffeine.

I missed having the freedom to take a hot bath for longer than five minutes. I missed hearing myself talk when someone called me on the phone. Being a stay-at-home mom was rewarding, but if I were honest, I did feel isolated. Most of my friends chose to work as they raised their babies. When we weighed it out, my measly income would basically help with my car payment and day-care costs. I was dedicated to raising our baby full-time. We wanted to have a family for so long I just couldn't bear the thought of missing my baby's firsts. First smile, first tooth, first step, and first word. I wanted to be the one to hold him when he needed consoling, to kiss his boo-boos, and to teach him right from wrong. I persevered and stuck to my guns and realized the true value of a stay-at-home parent. In our culture, it's not uncommon to feel insignificant when someone asks you, "So what do you do?" I used to get so frustrated because I know many people assumed it was easy to be a stay-at-home mom. The experience is far from sitting on the couch eating bonbons!

One of my friends admitted she had to go back to work. She had postpartum depression and needed to put her baby in day care. I get it! But that did make me so sad. Forgive me for being old-fashioned, but I used to be contemptuous to mothers who chose to work or follow a career over her child. Now I try not to criticize. Not everyone is meant to do what I felt so strongly about. In my opinion, having the responsibility of a job and being a mom is even more stressful and difficult. The small window of quality time is almost impossible! I'm just so thankful I was given the ability to stay home with our baby. Some moms don't have a choice.

In the beginning, I actually felt like a freeloader. A moocher off my husband. I know that sounds terrible, but I was used to contributing financially or at least helping with the businesses. I didn't know how to relax without feeling like I was viewed as lazy. When Herb came home from work, he learned the worst question he could ask me was, "So what did you do today?" I felt like I was being interrogated and that I needed to fill out a work-order form and list all my accomplishments. Even though I cleaned throughout the day, by the time hubby came home, you couldn't tell.

Motherhood isn't something you can master. It takes years of learning, and just when you think you've got the hang of it, something else throws you for a loop!

I went through the challenges of supplementing formula because I felt like my baby was hungry. I was disappointed that I went that route because Little Herbie went through a difficult time while we were experimenting formulas. We tried a couple different ones, but he was having serious reactions. We had to book an appointment with a pediatric gastroenterology physician.

Once he could eat applesauce, bananas, and cereal, it got much easier for both of us. I recorded the precious moments in his baby book: when he would nibble on his toes and hold his own bottle; the times I would put him on the phone with his Auntie Keri, and he would giggle; his first haircut and his first happy meal; him grabbing the tail of our cat, Willie; him blowing bubbles; and that one time he ate his crayons.

I know we were considered overly protective parents. The evidence was obvious. The entire house was baby-proofed to create a safer environment. We bought all the essentials. We covered the electrical outlets, locked kitchen cabinets, and drawers were fastened with plastic latches. We didn't take any chances and made sure large furniture items were bolted to the walls. You hear of all the worst-case scenarios, and you want to make sure the worst can be prevented. Little Herbie was about six months old when we were watching the news one evening and noticed the announcement of the largest recall in national history. There were over fifty million window blinds that were being recalled. A mom expressed the loss of her child to a cord from a window blind that was accessible to the baby. The crib was next to the window, and the child was strangled by the inner cord. I was frantic and so livid. I was ignorant and had no idea that my window blinds had the potential to hurt our child. My heart hurt for the mom who advocated awareness and fought to be heard. Immediately we removed the window blinds from the baby's room and the rest of the house.

Then I gave it some thought while my husband and baby were sound asleep. I was rummaging through some plastic parts till 2:00

a.m., trying to come up with a contraption that would help minimize or eliminate any further loss of lives. I was outraged that it is estimated that every two weeks, a child dies from the dangers of window blinds. Why wasn't anyone doing something about this horrific tragedy? The thought came to me, *Why don't you do something?* It became my mission as a mom to spread awareness to other moms and parents that had mini blinds in their homes. The more I did research, the more I became obsessed. I woke Herb up around 3:00 a.m., proudly displaying my newfound remedy. With some manipulation, Herb and I devised an idea of a small invention that we believed could be a solution to the problem. It was basically a small plastic device that you could wind up the entire length of the cord clockwise around the spool of a plastic base. You would lock the cord in the L-shaped slot and firmly press the suction cup to the highest part of the window. If you used our product in conjunction with the hold-down brackets from the manufacturer of the window blinds, even the inner cord would be secured, giving optimal safety results.

I asked my friend Tina if she thought her husband could help draw up some plans. We needed blueprints, and he was an engineer. He was kind enough to help us on our quest. We didn't have any experience, but we knew a lot of people who could point us in the right direction. We were enthusiastic about our new product and pursued a patent. We paid a small fee with the United States Patent Office and were officially patent pending! We reached out to an artist in East Brookfield to create a logo: a husband-and-wife team that has been in business for years. Talented and very nice people. They were so supportive and helpful. We wanted to make the product for both animals and children because the more we did research, the more we realized deaths were not just happening to children. Cats were getting tangled and trapped in the long cords as well. We didn't have the financial means to front this operation, but Herb said, "Kristi, even if we save just one child's life, it's worth it." I agreed; there's no price that can compare to the value of a loved one. Over a period of time, we invested tens of thousands of dollars.

We even met up with another couple from our church for additional advice with our finances, a separate issue that we were still working on. We were grateful for Harold and Jane Harper, but we were in search for more advice preferably from the perspective of married business owners. This married couple were successful local business owners; we wanted to learn the ropes from someone who had similar beginnings that didn't have a weekly paycheck from an employer. Marco and Ginny were very nice to welcome us into their home and go over our finances. We were so eager to share our plans and goals with them. Because they were successful and started from the ground up, we wanted to become teachable and learn from them. We were ready to take notes if they were willing to reveal their secrets to success. We laid out the assets and liabilities, the expenses, and the income, looking for wisdom and guidance. Toward the end of our visit, I shared our invention with them and was superpassionate about the product and our hopes.

We didn't get any advice or direction from Marco and Ginny on our current finances, but we did get a phone call saying they believed in our invention and wanted to generously give us money to further our desire for a patent. I was so overwhelmed and taken off guard. I was emotional and couldn't believe that they wanted to invest in us and our vision. They said they didn't want anything in return, that it would be a gift. The goal was to get the patent with the help from Marco and Ginny. They felt like God gave us this idea, and they wanted to see us climb out of the debt. Maybe this product would do just that? We accepted their offer but told them we wouldn't have been able to continue on without their support. We wanted to honor them by making them 50 percent silent partners. We were hoping that since this couple knew how to run things, they would be able to give us advice. We were hoping they would mentor us in the process since they had so much experience and success.

With Little Herbie on my hip, I was in between mothering and this new endeavor. I felt like the cause was worthy of my attention and time. We were meeting with plastic companies and creating an injection mold. What a fulfilling feeling.

As you already know, Herb has two brothers, and I have a twin sister and a younger brother. We both have two siblings, which can come in handy when you need someone to pin the blame on. How difficult it must be to be an only child. When we used to talk about the magic number of kids we both wanted, we agreed three was a good number. We wanted a sibling for our little monkey. Don't ask me why I didn't think God could provide us with another miracle; maybe I thought it was rude or ungrateful to even think of asking God for another child. So we decided to recertify our classes with MAPP. After completing the course, we were delighted to find out we were pregnant again! How hysterical is that? I can't make this stuff up! It was July 28, 2010, that we announced Little Herbie was going to be a big brother! This time, we didn't require the assistance of fertility specialists. No drugs, no ovulation-predictor kits—we were naturally conceiving! Wow!

This pregnancy was very different from the last one with Little Herbie. First of all, naps were creatively planned simultaneously when I put Herbie down. Yes, I was drained, but that was becoming the new normal. This time, I was chasing a toddler. I was so thankful I only gained forty pounds. Being less heavy allowed me more mobility, and I needed it. My honey and I agreed not to find out the gender. Since this pregnancy was so different from my first, I would have bet I was going to have a baby girl.

Surprisingly, I was wrong! March 21, 2011, 8:40 a.m., Benjamin William Seymour claimed his place in the world. I don't know why, but our babies weren't small! He was nine pounds, eleven ounces, and twenty-one inches long. He had dark-blue eyes, light-brown hair, and the loudest cry I ever heard! The resemblance was astounding to his big brother. He could have passed as his brother's twin. I needed another cesarean section. No difficulties with feeding him like I had with Little Herbie, thank God!

It wasn't easy juggling two strong-willed boys, but my goodness was it a fun time. Cuteness overload! We proudly picked the name *Benjamin* for multiple meaningful reasons: Benjamin is a strong biblical name. The Hebrew-origin meaning is "son of my right hand." I love that! Also, my sister's appointed name that was given to her when she became a nun was Sister Benjamin. Thirdly, it also happens to be Herb's grandfather's name on his mother's side. This child had no fear. He was our wild child. He loved to dance to music and was always so happy. He was very ticklish, and his laugh was contagious. Benjamin was an economical child. We saved everything that belonged to Little Herbie, and we were able to reuse it. Since Benjamin had an older brother, it seemed he was learning things a lot faster for his age. We noticed his adorable underbite and gave him the endearing nickname "Benny the Bulldog." Now we had a monkey and a bulldog.

Welcome

Share your food with the hungry and give shelter to the homeless. Give clothes to those who need them, and do not hide from relatives who need your help.

—Isaiah 58:7 NLT

Our home was quite full by this point. Maybe our lifestyle dreams of the Waltons were coming true after all. Every inch of the square footage in our home was occupied. My mom was thankfully in remission from Graves' disease, still living with us. She sacrificially opted to move in the downstairs area so her brother (my uncle Mark) and Herb's mom could move in. Unfortunate events took place, and they were unable to afford the home we built for them a couple miles down the road from us. My mom's sister and her husband (my aunt and uncle) also needed a place to stay. Thanksgiving Day, they were struggling and upset with their current living arrangements, so we offered them a place to stay at one of our rental homes. It was right on the lake in Spencer. It was a beautiful spot. My cousin that had been living in our basement apartment (the same one Misty and Ray used to live in) was going through a divorce, a much unexpected one to say the least; they were newly married. But he asked Herb and I if he could swap into the lake house, he would give his place to my aunt and uncle. And so, with all the shuffling, that's exactly what happened.

Over the years, Herb and I had a heart for someone who needed a place to land. We know how expensive it is out there for apartments and how difficult it can be to wait for a place. We've even taken in a former employee when he was going through hard times. Herb and

I laugh now, but there was a time Tony was there, and Herb was searching for batteries. You might have thought Herb was the guest because he didn't know where to find any double As. Tony confidently pointed Herb to the middle drawer of our hutch. He knew exactly where we kept the them.

With two little ones, it was getting more challenging to host Bible studies. We loved being hospitable and having people over, but I was unable to participate as much as I wished I could. Many people would fill our kitchen table with their Bibles and desserts. The times were memorable. We had a lot of genuine conversation and learned a great deal. Pastor Ron and Sherry were investing in us and mentoring us. We were maturing in Jesus and growing in our faith.

For years, we had different kinds of studies, from the book of Acts to Dave Ramsey's Financial Peace University. We were hungry for knowledge, and many family members were beginning to see what we were a part of was real. At first, many friends and family alike would josh us and ask if we joined a cult. We couldn't help but laugh because we knew we probably would have thought the same thing! So many mysteries were being revealed to us through these gatherings. We had the joy of witnessing many loved ones surrender their lives to Jesus. The power of God worked through us and others, and it was evident. Herb's Auntie Joanie came right up to us and asked us what it was that we were on. She said our faces were glowing. We gave all the credit to the One who is deserving. We shared with her that we have Jesus. She didn't hesitate and said she wanted Jesus too!

Uncle Tony would make the same decision as well. And then came Uncle Tony's mom and dad, Pat and Rico. The Holy Spirit was spreading like wildfire. Another significant and profound day for me was when my mom held hands at our table and repeated the sinner's prayer after Pastor Ron prompted an invitation. She allowed Jesus to reign in her life. Satan didn't win my family. We had victory in Jesus!

Do you remember when I articulated my vivid dream earlier? It occurred to me years later that my vision was fulfilled. Physical buildings didn't crumble around me, but my concern of what would happen to my husband and my mother disappeared. I now knew without a doubt their eternal life was sealed with Christ. The day they are called away from this world, they will reside in heaven with Jesus. That gave me an insurmountable amount of peace. Fear of death was replaced with confidence in the promises of those who believe in Christ. I was beyond grateful that God allowed me that gift. I had the privilege of witnessing both my husband and my mother confess Jesus as their Lord and Savior.

It didn't just happen at our kitchen table; it was happening everywhere! Even if I went for a walk, I would share my testimony with anyone who was willing to listen. Don't get me wrong, there were many times I would share the truth with others, and they refused to take any steps closer. Yes, they did reject Jesus, but I learned over time not to take it personally. My job is to share, love, and pray. It's God's job to do the rest. I wasn't afraid of following up with some people to ask them if they wanted to talk more about our previous conversation.

There are so many opportunities these days to reach out to others. I've been open even to reach out by computer. I later found out my high school friend Emma responded to Jesus through an e-mail I sent to her. Don't limit what God can do. I'm certainly no Billy Graham, but I do believe God gives all His children the ability to evangelize and share the good news with anybody.

What better place to walk someone to Jesus than in a procession line at a funeral? Yup, you heard that right! Even during intense grief, God may use you in the most bizarre moments. Yes, it was awkward, but I was obedient to God and prayed with a distant family member and led her to Christ. It wasn't long after she died of cancer. God's timing is intentional. The stories are numerous. Nothing brings me greater joy than someone saying yes to God. Did you know in Luke 15:10, the Bible says, "In the same way, there is joy in the presence of God's angels when even one sinner repents." Sounds like an angelic party, if you ask me!

I depend on the Holy Spirit to guide my words when I share with others. Some people I am gentle and cautious with, and others I am feisty and audacious. One time my cousin Erika was helping me clean a house for a few extra bucks. I remember sharing with her my testimony and explaining God's goodness in my life. Yes, this is the same Erika I spoke of earlier in my book. At this point, she's no longer a child. We have a mutual love for each other, and over the years, I've tried to be a good example for her and an encourager. At the end of my conversation with her, I asked her where she stands. She said she knows what I say is true, that she can't deny God's hand in my life, but she refused to make a commitment to follow Him. Something in my spirit rose up, and I explained to her that her decision to wait and push aside Jesus has the exact same consequences as someone who hates God. I gave her the example of a well-known anti-Christ artist. I urged her to understand that the severity of her refusal to welcome Jesus into her life would be the same fate as the person who worships Satan. After I said those words with authority and conviction, I thought to myself how harsh that must have sounded. But I trusted it was what she was meant to hear. It would be years later that she wholeheartedly received Jesus as her Lord and Savior through a close friend God had put into her life. It's not important to me who gets the honor of "closing the deal"; all that matters to me is that they do.

Here's another learning experience for me. Christian programming often ran on our television. Herb's mom popped in to visit, and we were watching a well-known televangelist speak of the importance of repenting from your sins and receiving the eternal gift of salvation through Jesus Christ. The speaker was calling people in the audience to come to the front of the room and make the decision if they felt led by God to pray and ask Jesus into their hearts. This is by far one of my favorite moments to watch as people of all races, ethnicity, and gender gather together and make the commitment to repeat the prayer. I was trying to explain what the audience was doing when Denise (my mother-in-law) was watching the TV. I was narrating the program in full detail. I thought the program required explanation. God wasn't in need of my two cents. I had no idea I was interrupting her moment with God. Basically, I was told to shut up and that she was trying to pray the prayer for herself! Unintentionally at times, when I believe I'm being helpful, I'm actually getting in the way. I happily shut my mouth and thanked God that He was using our television as an opportunity for Herb's mom to belong to God. It reminded me to stop and listen. I don't always need to say something. The last thing I want to hear from God is that I was the cause of a distraction from someone who was being called to Him.

We were learning a lot during church, but we found a small-group Bible study was beneficial to growing our knowledge in a more intimate and personal way. We could bounce questions around the table and get multiple perspectives from faithful followers who had more experience and wisdom. Maybe you already knew this, but we learned *Christ* was not Jesus's last name; it is the official title of our Lord. Back in those days, Jesus was a common name just like *Bob*, *Mike*, or *Bill* is today. Christ comes from the Greek word *Christos*; it means "anointed one" or "messiah" in Hebrew. The Chosen One by God. The One who was foretold, prophesied.

Many revelations were learned at our kitchen table. God was invited center-stage. We prayed a lot, and individually we all could ask for specific prayer requests. We loved having a safe environment that we could share important life lessons with where we didn't feel criticized. We felt empowered by having a community of family that loved God and loved us unconditionally. We were told truth in love. There was no small talk. We didn't focus on the weather and sports. We talked about life-changing matters that made an impact for our future. It was refreshing. We were challenged to renew our minds in Christ.

I remember one time when I asked Pastor Ron about our experience in the past when we went to see Madam Jean. I asked him how was it possible that a stranger had the ability to see the events of our future. I shared the details of the things she said specifically with the motorcycle and septic issues. When he began to reveal the truth to me, it actually made sense! I'll try to convey what he said to the best of my ability. He clarified to me that just as there are angels in the spirit realm, there are also fallen angels. One-third of the fallen angels chose to follow Satan (the devil) and were thrown out of heaven to earth. They are called demons. He described that these demons have been on this earth for thousands of years. Their goal is to ultimately win as many souls away from God as they can. They hate God, and therefore, they hate humankind because we are made in God's image.

These demons have powers and abilities to make things occur. When we seek fortune-tellers and mediums, we are giving Satan and his demons permission to come into our lives. If a woman has a gift to see into the future, she either receives that gift from God and can prophesy for God, or she receives the power from Satan to further his dominion. Demons can whisper to the fortune-teller things only you may know because they are present and can see and study our behaviors. They know our weaknesses. Not only that, they have been following our ancestors, so they know more about us and our temptations than we do!

Basically, because we went to that fortune-teller many years ago, the demons that assisted her were possibly given permission through our ignorance to make the future events like our septic problems happen. It is very important that we rebuke the demons and ask Jesus to cover our past errors. It is also important that we renounce any authority that we willingly participated that opened doors to the enemy. With respect for Jesus, we do not practice or participate in spiritual evil. You won't find a Magic 8-Ball in my home. We don't mess with ouija boards, horror movies, dream catchers, tarot cards, horoscopes, or anything that glorifies Satan. We refuse to allow Satan and his demons the ability to trespass into our lives. Early in our walk with God, we were so protective I admit for the longest time I was even paranoid over opening a tiny fortune cookie!

We noticed when we cleansed our home of things that didn't honor God, we were at peace and even slept better!

What is 99 percent truth? I loved when Pastor Ron would ask people that. The bottom line is, 99 percent of the truth is still a lie! I believe that is why many people are so easily deceived. Being a stay-at-home mom was isolating for sure. I pitied Jehovah's Witnesses knocking on my door. I used to kindly reject them and send them on their way. Not anymore! One day, a kind, timid woman named Rachel knocked on my front door. I'm pretty sure she had no idea what she was getting herself into! I welcomed her in and offered her coffee—she and her well-dressed bodyguards! I wasn't intimidated at all. I shared my testimony confidently with her and graciously pointed to the truth. We kept in contact. I wrote her a couple of letters in hopes that God would renew her mind to His truth and free her from the lie she was serving. My thoughts were, *If you really believe God loves you and that you belong to Him, why are you so afraid?* She seemed to be scared and didn't have a peaceful demeanor. Did she think she was earning her ticket to heaven? The Jesus she believed in certainly wasn't the same Jesus that I knew. His blood on the cross proved His perfect unconditional love for me. It is sufficient to pay for all my sins.

There's no way I would believe God would only choose 144,000 people to be with Him in paradise while billions of souls are unknowingly predestined for hell. It's so sad; Jehovah's Witnesses seem to be some of the nicest people. They go door to door believing their actions will bless others. They have a point system in place when they can leave literature with unsuspecting homeowners. But the bottom line is, you can't omit truth from the Bible to make it fit your agenda. It's not the whole truth! Many will be led astray. The consequences will be inevitable to those who are responsible. We have to remember Satan is the father of lies. He twists the truth. He is a counterfeit. It is our responsibility to pay attention with discernment and not be lured away by half-truths. After all, that is exactly how Eve was tempted in the garden. Satan questioned Eve, got her to engage in conversation, and ultimately brought death to humankind. Don't be fooled by his smooth tongue. He comes to steal, kill, and destroy!

Don't just believe everything someone tells you, including myself! Do your own research. Ask more than one trustworthy person. Pray for clarity and discernment. Back it up with scripture from the Bible.

Maybe you're wondering what the importance of this "Bible" is? Why should I believe anything that is printed in this book? What makes it so special? Those are all reasonable questions. We learned a lot on the validity of the Bible. How old and reliable it is and who wrote it. I am convinced only because God has blessed me with unshakeable faith that the Bible is the written Word of God. Over the years as I have read it, the pages have come alive for me in a personal way. I can testify that many of my deep, soul-searching questions have been answered through the words in this book that is holy.

It truly is a love letter from God to His people. It was all foreign to me before I knew Christ. I tried to read it before, and I couldn't grasp anything. I was frustrated when I attempted to read it, so I gave up trying.

Here are a few reasons why I believe the Bible is the Word of God: If I may make a suggestion, do some of your own digging and research for yourself why the Bible is a trusted resource. I was fascinated when I found out the Bible was written over a span of approximately 1,500 years by forty different authors. That impressed me because many people attest to events that took place with their own personality coming through the pages. There is no discrepancy in the details. Also, the Bible fulfills prophecy (predicts the future) in very specific ways. The Bible has been arguably the most historically accurate book than any other ancient book. There is scientific and archeological evidence that proves the Bible's reliability. Archeologists are still making new discoveries that prove that the Bible stories most of us have heard of as children are not just cute fables. Imagine that! Second Timothy 3:16–17 NLT says, "All Scripture is inspired by God and is useful to teach us what is true and to make us realize what is wrong in our lives. It straightens us out and teaches us to do what is right. It is God's way of preparing us in every way, fully equipped for every good thing God wants us to do." What I do know is from experience. Without supernatural intervention from God, the Bible cannot be fully understood. There are so many other people who are qualified to give better information than I can. That's about as theological as I am equipped.

Another eye-opener for me was when I was reading Genesis 28:10–13 NIV:

> Jacob left Beersheba and set out for Harran. When he reached a certain place, he stopped for the night because the sun had set. Taking one of the stones there, he put it under his head and lay down to sleep. He has a dream in which he saw a stairway resting on the earth, with its top reaching to heaven, and the angels of God were

ascending and descending on it. There above it stood the Lord, and he said: I am the Lord, the God of your father Abraham and the God of Isaac. I will give you and your descendants the land on which you are lying.

When I read this, my heart pounded hard. I had recalled years ago, when Herb's dad passed away as he sat in his recliner in the living room, that Herb's mom shared an interesting experience with me. I admit I had a difficult time believing her. She told me that before Dad took his last breath, she saw a stairway to heaven with angels on it, and she was also standing on the stairs. Dad was unsure of the female who greeted him. He couldn't recognize her. Denise told him, "Call out to Jesus and go with the woman." Dad kept repeating the word *Jesus* over and over again until he was taken. The specific details she shared with me were undoubtedly the same account that Jacob describes. I was in awe. For me, it confirmed again that this heavenly realm is, in fact, a real place.

Perfect Strangers

God has given each of you a gift from his great variety of spiritual gifts. Use them well to serve one another.

—1 Peter 4:10 NLT

In my high school years, when I rode the bus to school, I used to gaze out my window at the houses we would pass by. One log cabin on my left caught my attention often. There was nothing overly fancy about it, but I used to wonder what the interior looked like. Taking up fashion design was a fitting trade for my mentality.

The log cabin was charming. It was nestled within the trees of a heavily wooded lot a little way beyond the main road. It was small and simple. The front porch was welcoming, and it looked like it dated back to the pioneer days. It wasn't until roughly fifteen years later I would develop a beautiful relationship with the owner of that exact location! Happenstance? Nah! Her name is Drew Hicks. She is a vivacious woman with tawny auburn hair and ocean-blue smiling eyes. She and I were introduced at a physical therapy office out in Sturbridge. My family and I visit her as frequently as we need to. You see, she is blessed with the gift of healing.

Drew Hicks is so humble and never claims glory for herself. She gives Jesus the credit while happily serving others who are in tremendous pain and through the most extraordinary methods. When you walk out of her tiny office space, the pain is gone! My husband can attest to this. I convinced him to try a session with her for his ankle. He had a fifteen-year-old sports injury. He told me when he went to see her, she began evaluating his posture and told him he was way "off." I already knew that! She began working on his shoulder area when he interrupted her to remind her that the swelling and inflammation was in his ankle. She nodded and proceeded to work on his upper body. When he stepped out of her office, he was a believer! The relief was immediate and undeniable. Clearly, what took place was nothing short of supernatural!

What I find fascinating is when she can read my body like a puzzle. She could tell if I was slouching in the fetal position on my Papasan chair or if I was sitting like a mermaid with both legs to one side on the couch. This body is a tattletale! She usually could determine if you took a fall or had an injury even if you didn't disclose that information. Impressive, if you ask me! Over the years, I've considered her to be more like a friend or an "older" sister in Christ. Yes, it just so happens she loves Jesus too! She not only puts my body back together after many months of abuse, but she is also an encourager and lifts my spirits. She listens well, is generous with her time, and offers advice only if you ask. There are times I feel God's presence so strongly when I'm with her; it moves us both to tears. She's not afraid to get real. To be vulnerable and professional at the same time is a fine line that she masters. There's so much that happens when I'm lying on her massage table. We laugh, pray, and cry together. It's a beautiful thing! We exchange meaningful music, movies, and homesteading tips. When I close my eyes, even though she is in the room with me, I can go to a deep state of meditation—that is, if she's not chewing gum! I hear quiet music playing in the background from a choice playlist she preprogrammed for her clients and her soft breathing. My life is richer with Drew Hicks.

That reminds me of a short story. There's only one time I was aware that God used me supernaturally to heal anyone in my life. I went to a women's retreat one weekend with the ladies from my church and asked the assistant pastor's wife, Bonnie, why she hadn't been on the worship team in a while. She said something was going on with her voice and that she went to the doctor's for her symptoms. I told her I believed she was under spiritual attack and hastily put my hand on her throat as I said a quick prayer in the name of Jesus. After I did it, I felt a bit embarrassed (I don't know how I would feel if someone just took ahold of my throat). I found myself apologizing. Even though I believe in miracles, I was even surprised when she pulled out her guitar and sang that weekend! Either she wasn't in shock like I was, or she could contain her composure better than me. She never mentioned another thing about it. I asked Jesus for forgiveness; I really expected acknowledgement, at least maybe even a thank-you. Then I realized I was still immature in my walk because I was a "glory seeker." That's probably why God never used me again like that! You really have to be a person of great humility!

As for the interior of Drew Hicks's home? I had the pleasure of seeing it a few times. The home did not disappoint my expectations. She had a knack for primitive decor and lots of furry friends inside and outdoors. Love resided there.

Another special woman God put in my life at the time I needed her most was my friend Mary. We became acquainted at my church. She was best known as the "baby whisperer." Every Sunday she was cradling someone's baby during church services. She loved children. She understood my fears and waited patiently to earn my trust. I wasn't the kind of mom who felt very comfortable allowing just anyone to hold my baby. It didn't take long for me to love Mary. She was a stern woman and demanded respect. She was a breath of fresh air. She stepped up and offered to do just about anything that would help ease the burden. She would clean my floors (not with a mop, she was old-school) on her hands and knees with a rag. She would bake treats with the boys or just offer to babysit so my honey and I could have a much-needed date night.

She took the time to call, and if I didn't answer my phone, she would leave me the most endearing messages on my voice mail. She reached out regularly. She used to call me "sweet girl." God, I miss her! She was sarcastic, loved to smoke cigarettes, and when she laughed, she cackled with a deep, hoarse, raspy voice. I envied her; she was practically thirty years older than me and had twice the level of my energy. She loved her coffee. I learned a lot of valuable lessons from her. She woke up daily to serve others. She was sacrificial. She worked in pain and wouldn't complain even if the pain was excruciating. She didn't let it stop her. That was her mission: to be useful and help others. As much as I thought I was special to her, she didn't play favorites; she was a butterfly. She would help many others in the body of Christ. If she didn't have our kids, she had Pastor Kole and Bonnie's kids; and if she didn't have their kids, she had someone else's kids. She loved her neighbors, knew many by name, floated in and out of the lives of many people over the handful of years I got to know her personally. I miss her sticky lipstick kisses on my cheek and her scrawny hugs.

I can still remember going to her house, smelling her fresh laundry hanging outside on the clothesline. She would feed the raccoons and tend to her flower gardens by her side entry. She managed a lot for one woman. She made sure to remind me how much God loves me. She did have a gift for words of affirmation. And if you asked her how she was doing, she used to always say, "It is well with my soul." And while she babysat the kids, she warned them, "No boo-boos on my watch!"

Sometimes I think she knew her days were coming to an end. She returned an item I gave to her shortly before she died. She wanted to make sure to return it to me. At first, I was insulted; now I treasure that item even more than I did before. My boys will never forget the crockagators that swam by the river next to her home (she was a storyteller). And I'll never forget the love she poured out onto my family. I still make her famous salad with cranberries and toasted slivered almonds, and I'm thankful I have her carrot cake recipe. Even though I may come close, it will never taste exactly the same. But most of all, I will cherish the memories my boys spent with her. She would allow them (as little as they were) to sit on top of her kitchen countertops, whip up a dessert, and help her bake something yummy. She would let them stick their tiny fingers in the batter and lick the bowl as their little legs would dangle over the side.

Just as she went house to house helping anyone who would receive her, so did her stainless steel cooking pot make frequent visits to multiple homes, full of the best soups and homemade meals. It was no surprise it was her wish to be cremated when she passed on. She wasn't an extravagant woman, but I didn't expect her ashes would be held in her stainless steel cooking pot during the funeral! I couldn't help but laugh when Pastor Ron pointed to the pot and told everyone that was her request—to be put in that pot! That goes to show you her sense of humor!

Sometimes when we stroll through her hometown, we'll take her road, but it's not the same. Her home is gone from the premises. Completely demolished and removed. There is no evidence of her perennials or gardens. It's all gone. But her memory will remain close to my heart until we are together again. I never got to say goodbye. Maybe that was the way she would have wanted it. Sometimes I ask Jesus to give her a big squeeze from me and tell her that I love and miss her terribly!

Uprooted

So, I turned in despair from hard work. It was not the answer to my search for satisfaction in this life. For though I do my work with wisdom, knowledge and skill, I must leave everything I gain to people who haven't worked to earn it. This is not only foolish but highly unfair. So, what do people get for all their hard work? Their days of labor are filled with pain and grief; even at night they cannot rest. It is all utterly meaningless.

—Ecclesiastes 2:20–23 NLT

With an adjustable mortgage rate breathing down our necks and the value of our home decreasing over one hundred thousand dollars, we were unable to refinance. Most of our tenants stopped paying their rent, and we couldn't front any more of our own money on our investment properties. We were stuck. We felt defeated.

A good friend of ours worked in the collections department at a bank. We openly shared our money concerns with our group. She was coming to our weekly Financial Peace University classes at our home and offended us with her honesty. As much as I didn't want to agree with what she said, she was right, and I was in denial. She bluntly mentioned that we just couldn't afford our home anymore.

Sherry made a remark as well. She asked us hypothetically, if God ever asked us to let go of our home, would we? That question rubbed me the wrong way. How could anyone ask such a thing? Don't they know all the trials, difficulties, and years of suffering we went through to get this home? Stubbornly, I refused the thought of ever giving up on our home. Not gonna happen—no way, no how! Then she said, "Kristi, what if this house has already served its purpose?" That was a perspective I never gave much thought.

We were weighing out our options and procrastinating the inevitable. We were struggling with the consequences of a bad handshake years ago. Jesus might have forgiven us of all our past sins, but that didn't mean we weren't going to suffer the effects.

My honey couldn't work any harder. There were times he would come home late nights exhausted. One day when he came home around 11:00 p.m., he was filthy from the trade and plopped himself on the couch. (The company that bought out our business went under and threatened to lay off one of Herb's former employees, who followed Herb to the new company. Herb interceded on his friend's behalf and told the company to spare the guy, that Herb could always go back into business now that the no-compete clause was null and void.) It was like he was in a trance, staring off into the distance. Then he desperately looked at me and said, "Kristi, I just can't do this anymore!" He wanted to be a good provider for our children and support our household. And even though we had some financial help from family, it wasn't enough. I comforted my husband and told him I didn't care if we had to pitch a tent, that his well-being was worth more to me than a house made of wood. I supported him in his decision to give it up. We did it for each other. We did it for our babies. We remembered that when we filed for bankruptcy a couple years prior, our lawyer included our mortgage. So if we walked away, technically we wouldn't be responsible.

I used to cry watching Little Herbie stand patiently (in nothing but a diaper) peering out of our glass door waiting for his daddy to come home. This wasn't fair to our babies. They wanted their daddy. This wasn't the way we envisioned life as a family. Nothing material mattered to us anymore. I'm not saying it was an easy decision because it wasn't. But at what cost were we willing to stay?

I passionately hate the 1974 folk rock song "Cats in the Cradle" by Harry Chapin. It is a story of a father-and-son relationship. At first, the father misses his child's first steps while he is out providing for his family. Then the son looks up to his dad and keeps asking his father, "When you coming home, Dad?" But the dad doesn't have a clear answer to the boy, who desires to spend time together. The dad continues to push his boy aside and doesn't make it a priority to teach him how to throw a ball. But the son still worships his father and says one day he's gonna be just like his dad. Then as the boy grows up, he loses interest in spending time with his dad. He'd rather borrow his dad's car and leave. Then as the son becomes a father, he repeats the cycle that he was taught and is too busy to visit his retired father. Life gets in the way. I think the reason I hate this song so much is the fact that there is so much truth in it. We all have desires to connect with loved ones, and for one reason or another, it becomes more complicated than it should. It's easy to take for granted that the option will always be available. What if it isn't? Truly, it is one of the saddest songs in my opinion.

Our home was no longer an idol. We felt unexplainable freedom. The next day, we literally put everything we had on the front lawn and held the largest yard sale. We had a lot of possessions and wanted to downsize. Our living-room set and kitchen table were out on the front lawn with many other collectibles from over the years. It was kind of funny when the neighbors told us they felt guilty for buying our stuff. Rumors were spreading fast. I even heard through the grapevine that Herb and I were in the middle of a divorce! One of the most heart-wrenching steps that had to be taken were when we had to present our decision to the entire household. We knew our decision hinged on the lives of many loved ones. Herb insisted that he tell everyone alone since he was the man of the house. We didn't know what to expect. We didn't know if there would be shouting and arguments, and we didn't want our children to witness a potential catastrophe. We just couldn't bear the weight any longer. Now that we had children, our priorities changed. We had no intention of hurting anyone, but that's exactly what happened. Gossip was flying all over the place, and no matter how much we tried to communicate, our once-peaceful home was in disarray.

Not only were we losing our dream home, we were losing the very people closest to us. Great misunderstanding hovered over us all. No matter how many times we tried to explain that this was a financial crisis, it didn't matter. Emotions took over. Things were said that I won't repeat. Feelings were crushed. Everything spiraled downhill. Family even thought at one point we premeditated and conspired this idea for months. They assumed we had a backup plan and a house to go to. We didn't.

I made promises I couldn't keep. I felt like a failure. But just as much as I depended on God to supply our needs, I prayed He would supply all their needs too.

It got ugly. It was so hard for me because I wanted to defend ourselves. Holidays were painful. I never knew what it felt like to be the black sheep of the family till then. We suffered a lot.

I felt suppressed. I tried to restrain from reacting. Often I needed to vent, but I didn't want our children to hear me. I didn't want their perception of the family to be tainted because of my hurt. I felt so ostracized, shunned, blacklisted. I couldn't believe the way we were all behaving. Yes, I admit I played a part in all of this. I showcased being a victim; I'm not proud of that. I was so disappointed that no one called me and my husband to see how we were. No one called us to even ask for our side of the story. I was told week after week some family members would congregate together and complain about the raw deal they were given. I heard stuff like, we threw them out, or they were being evicted. I was so disappointed and disgusted. No one had our back. No one advocated for us. Instead of being grateful that we were able to help and house relatives (some for almost a decade), there was a spirit of entitlement. No one remembered the reasons that caused them to need a place to stay in the first place! Frankly, they were adults, and it wasn't my or my husband's responsibility or obligation.

I remember feeling rejected when we first came to Jesus. That was strange, but then again, Jesus's own words say in John 15:18, "If the world hates you, remember that it hated me first." I don't usually struggle with confrontation. I like to communicate in hopes to solve problems before they are magnified and blown out of proportion. I prefer to get it all out on the table and hash it out as long as the end result is reconciliation. The worst way to engage in a disagreement for me is to have to tiptoe around passive-aggressive behaviors. I can't stand when we are disrespected, lied to, and made to feel disposable. I wish I could say we had that opportunity to be heard. Even in a court of law, you're allowed the opportunity to give your defense. Unfortunately, this went on for many years and caused a huge amount of damage.

God stripped us basically of everything except for each other. We had to start over. Yes, it was ultimately our decision to stay or go, but we knew we would be stolen from if we stayed. We didn't want to miss the quality time with our boys. I don't regret our decision even if it caused a tremendous amount of agony.

I found incentive to pursue a place for our family to live. We drove around a lot searching for anything that we could afford. We lost all our investment houses and apartments to foreclosure. The bankruptcy destroyed our credit, and our options were slim. But we had faith. Herb asked me if I would be interested in looking at a mobile home in Brookfield. Immediately I said no. I needed God to gently pluck any pride that remained in me. I felt like I was being punished. How could we be reduced to a trailer again? It took us many years to graduate from a trailer only to end up exactly where we began. I did say I would move in a tent. I was being put to the test, and I detested it.

It wasn't my character, but I initiated a meeting with a nice lady from our church so I could take a peek at her mobile home. Something shifted and softened my heart. I met her at the place and looked around with our two boys. I was enchanted by its charm. It was quite cozy and clean. I saw the "For Sale" sign displayed on the front window, and can you believe two random women came inside asking to take a look around? I was getting competitive and jealous. Now that someone else was showing interest, I wanted it. The women asked if the kitchen table came with the sale. I wanted them to just leave! With a gracious smile, the lady from our church reassured me that if I was interested, not to worry; she would give me dibs. How sweet! Then it occurred to me, *What am I doing? I have no business shopping around! I don't have any money! Certainly not close to 40K!* It felt like she was reading my mind. She put me right at ease and asked me if I liked the home. I smiled and told her that I did. She asked me if we had a deposit. I shook my head no. She said, "Kristi, have your husband call my husband. I'm sure we can work something out." She told me that God nudged her to sell it, and she didn't know why. We both knew—it was because we were meant to be there! I was overflowing with great joy and appreciation.

After my honey called her husband, they agreed to allow us to move in and pay them as we could afford it. They even bargained a trade for some plumbing work in their new place so we could deduct it from the loan—churchgoers showing us the grace of God. We worked so hard that year, and the Lord provided us with enough money to pay them in ten months! Amazing!

The less we had, the more freedom we felt. We enjoyed our comfy home and found ourselves to be liberated. We stopped caring about what other people thought about us. We had no one to impress anymore. Our intimacy was stronger now that we had minimal expenses and overhead. Herb was spending more time with the boys, and we were digging out of debt. We borrowed an insane amount of money from Sean when times were good and the market was flourishing. When we listed all of our debts to the bankruptcy attorney, we omitted our agreement with Herb's brother out of love and respect even though by law we could have been cleared from it. We were faithfully chipping away at it. For years, we only could afford the interest payments; now we had hope to become free and keep our word. It felt really good. We knew if we stayed at our dream home, it would take us several years to pay the balance off. Proverbs 22:7 NLT says, "Just as the rich rule the poor, so the borrower is servant to the lender." It's hard to look someone in the eye when you owe them. It's a terrible feeling when you want to pay them, but you can't.

We had a tiny yard where we managed to squeeze in a vegetable garden, a secondhand swing set, and a kiddie pool. We had everything we needed. Our boys were happy and growing fast. Herb would even come home after work and find he had nothing to do! That never happened, so he used to help our elderly neighbors mow their lawns!

abundance

The Lord is my shepherd; I have all that I need. He lets me rest in green meadows; he leads me beside peaceful streams. He renews my strength. He guides me along right paths, bringing honor to his name. Even when I walk through the darkest valley, I will not be afraid, for you are close beside me. Your rod and your staff protect and comfort me. You prepare a feast for me in the presence of my enemies. You honor me by anointing my head with oil. My cup overflows with blessings. Surely your goodness and unfailing love will pursue me all the days of my life, and I will live in the house of the Lord forever.

—Psalm 23:1–6 NLT

Have you ever had a specific word stuck in your head and wondered where it came from? I kept repeating the word *abundance* in my mind over and over. I thought to myself, *How strange. It doesn't make any sense. Is there meaning behind it?* Then it dawned on me: March 27, 2013. With all that we gave up, God was giving us more! I found out I was pregnant again! It was equally as special as the first time I got pregnant. I put the positive pregnancy test on display with a paper that read "Abundance" on the kitchen table and waited for my honey to come home. Now that I had a little practice, I decided I wanted to record on video the moment when my husband came home and found out. His reaction was beautiful. He was surprised and gave me a huge hug. It's a joy that can't be fully explained.

The pregnancy was going well, but I did gain another sixty. I was so thankful I was always able to lose the weight after each delivery, even if it did take me some time. Little Herbie wasn't the only big brother anymore. We had personalized T-shirts made up for Herbie and Ben that read "Big Brother."

The boys were so much fun as they got to experience my belly grow. They loved to poke me and feel the baby kick and punch. It was rough being pregnant through the summer months. I swelled up, especially my ankles. Again, as tempted as we were to find out if this would finally be a baby girl, we waited. I can remember pulling the boys in a little red wagon up and down the sidewalks in our close-knit community. We would stroll to the postal area, and I would allow the boys to open our mailbox with the key and retrieve our mail. It was the little things they enjoyed.

The same friend of ours who had a knack for photography took some family maternity pictures nearby the pond. I wore a beautiful antique white lace dress that flaunted my oversized belly. The boys were in khaki shorts with spring-green short-sleeved flannel shirts, sporting their bare feet. My honey matched our handsome boys in similar attire. The boys had a net to catch critters from the pond. They seized an enormous bullfrog! This time, I had blonde tresses, a change from my natural brown. For some reason, our boys didn't seem to like cooperating whenever we attempted family portraits. As difficult as snapping the perfect shot was, Amanda got it! I gave dad a peck on his cheek as Little Herbie was on top of dad's shoulders. As pregnant as I was, I managed to balance Benjamin on top of my shoulders. Little Herbie was puckering up (while simultaneously smiling), leaning over as if he was going to smooch Benjamin while Benjamin's attention was 100 percent on the photographer, facing the camera with a smile from cheek to cheek. That is, by far, one of my most favorite pics! It reminds me of a modern version of a Norman Rockwell painting.

I'm definitely a picture person. I copied an awesome idea from Pinterest displaying various pictures. I have so many pictures of loved ones tacked up on a gingham fabric board in the hallway of our home. It's another visual reminder to pray for the people in our lives, past and present. It's my way of stopping to smell the roses. Sometimes I catch myself reminiscing.

Ready or not, here comes baby! My water broke unexpectedly. We had to round up the boys and my belongings. We dropped the boys off at Mimi and Puppa's apartment and headed off to the hospital. It was November 24, 2013, at 11:53 a.m. that Joseph Paul Seymour was born. I had my third Cesarean section. I was so convinced we were having a girl this time I brought pink baby clothes to the hospital along with blue (just in case). It was comical when we donated the pink items to the front desk of the maternity ward. The nurses thought it was funny when I told them I was convinced this pregnancy was so different from the first two that I was carrying a girl. I certainly was surprised, but not at all disappointed! I couldn't believe he was another ten-pounder! Ten pounds, one ounces, to be exact! He was twenty-one and a half inches long. He was so beautiful. He looked very similar to his brothers, with one exception. He had a cute little dimple on his left cheek, dark-brown eyes and brown hair. He had such a serious demeanor. I couldn't believe we had three sons! We chose the name *Joseph* for many reasons. Joseph means "He will add," and boy oh boy did He ever! We wanted to honor Uncle Nate by giving Joey his uncle's middle name *Paul*.

I was so happy when the doctor said we could take our newborn home on Thanksgiving Day! Just as I called my husband to arrange a ride home, the doctors came back into my room and said I was released to go but, they wanted to keep Joey for more tests. They informed me that our baby had a hole in his heart. Not at all what I expected. I was very upset, confused, and crying. I wished my husband could be with me and the baby, but he had to tend to our other children at home. This experience wasn't like my first two hospital stays; I definitely felt abandoned. I asserted that I would be staying with Joseph and asked my honey to put Joey on the prayer chain. If I recall correctly, the very next day, the hole closed up, and the heart murmur was gone. We were finally released to go home! Praise God!

This delivery took a toll on me. When I look back at pictures of this delivery, it caused me some concern. I noticed my husband's eyes weren't the same. He looked fearful. I asked him why, and he said, "We're done." I lost a lot of blood, and the doctors asked me for permission to allow them to give me a blood transfusion. With the effects of fifteen years of scar tissue from endometriosis, the laparoscopy and three C-sections (two that reopened the first every couple of years), I knew it probably wasn't safe to entertain the thought of having any more babies. I tried to enjoy this precious newborn, but I was already in a state of grief because I knew, most likely, this would be our last baby. It was bittersweet. I knew I needed to focus on being thankful that God allowed me to not only have one son but that He abundantly blessed us with three!

Whoever says having two is no more difficult than having three didn't know what they were talking about! I kind of felt bad for Joey. I wanted to cuddle him and hold him like I was able to with the other two but found it hard to give him the same attention. Someone was bound to get the shaft. Poor Dad. He was neglected often; we both were. There were times I felt incompetent because it was so difficult to juggle it all. Having number three (Joey) was totally different from having number one (Herbie) or number two (Ben), for that matter. The three-second rule came into play when binky fell on the floor. We didn't make a big deal about stuff that we used to. We had to learn how to pick our battles. We couldn't meet every demand on cue.

I loved the way the boys called Joseph *Jofish*. Now we had a monkey, a bulldog, and a fish! Perfect! The boys loved their baby brother. I tried to spread as much love as I could with the older two, especially so they wouldn't feel jealous. I praised them often and made sure I was meeting their needs to the best of my ability.

Joey shared our room for a little while. Now that we had three little ones, we were outgrowing the mobile home. We wanted a house with our own land, some privacy, and more room. The park was facing challenges of their own. What I assumed was mud that our boys were playing in turned out to be drainage from the septic right below the boys' swing set. It was time to hustle. Then when we found out a sex offender moved into a house in the park without registering—that was our final straw.

My honey promised me that he would give us a year before he made the appointment that would require him to sit with frozen peas. He didn't want to force me into that difficult decision. We both prayed and decided three was a perfect number. On Mother's Day, he blessed me with a ring he designed with a jeweler. Alexandrite, aquamarine, and citrine were the three stones that represented the birth months of the boys. Thoughtfully, he had bookended two diamonds to acknowledge the two babies we lost. He was always a meaningful gift giver. It was a moving and precious moment.

Herb had been in contact with a guy who's a little rough around the edges, but he had a heart for the less-fortunate. Herb took me for a ride in Warren to show me a cute gambrel-style house nestled in the woods near a dirt path. I remember he showed me this same house a while back, and it gave me the creeps because it was abandoned and needed a ton of work. But now it was sided, the overgrowth was trimmed, and it really had potential. When Herb took me and the boys inside, I fell in love with the kitchen. It was pretty. There was light-yellow paint on the walls, and there were custom-made shaker-style kitchen cabinets and tile floors. There were four bedrooms upstairs and two bathrooms! What I wouldn't give to have more than one bathroom again! There was a lot of privacy with a hiking trail behind the house. I could picture our family there. Herb would take a ride out to the property, bring his coffee early in the morning, and pray over it. He would ask God if there was a way that He would bless us with the house. He plucked a pinkish-purple flower from the rhododendron bush and brought it home to me.

Herb wanted the ability to give our family a home, so he made an offer to his buddy and explained the details of our situation. I couldn't believe he agreed to hold the mortgage for us for two years until we could get on our feet and get financing! The price was reasonable. Herb owed the man some plumbing favors. We were super-excited our boys would have a nice yard to play in, and we all would have plenty of space and privacy. The favor of God is wonderful.

There's something special about surprising the kids with a home of their own. I remember the day we took them there; they got to pick out their own rooms. Joey, being the baby, would be best next to the master bedroom. We allowed the boys to pick any color they wanted, and we painted their bedrooms. It was so exciting. We made this home a little homestead. Herb found an antique woodburning cookstove and grouted around the firewall that he installed in our kitchen. Now that we had the three in such a secluded spot, I felt it was important to have "bear" drills. There was no way I would be able to rescue three little ones quick enough. So I used to yell out, "It's an emergency!" The boys were trained. They knew that was their cue to run as fast as they could to the rear deck at our meeting place. Dad taught the boys how to shoot their BB guns and how to use a bow and arrow.

We had a pirate-themed birthday party for Little Herbie's sixth. Dad created swords from an old wooden picket fence, and we made a ship out of pallets. The sail came from an old white bedsheet. Many of Herbie's classmates from school joined in on the celebration. We greeted each child with a mustache, a black eye patch, and a scroll that opened into a treasure map. The treasure map was detailed with a red broken striped path that gave instructions and led them on the hunt from one destination to another. The X clearly marked the spot for treasure. Alligator alley (a huge green inflatable gator) was intended to intimidate the kids as they walked the plank. We even had a huge homemade palm tree as another landmark. We found an old vintage trunk that we filled with all kinds of toys, candy, and large fake gems. Forgive me for bragging, but I made an amazing cake! It was a giant treasure chest with a string of pearls and edible golden coins. We really outdid ourselves for this party on a modest budget. I admit, I had just as much fun as the kids did.

For my fortieth birthday, Herb surprised me with two fruit trees from the local orchard. I've always wanted an apple tree. The other fruit tree was peach. We planted gardens, bought the boys a trampoline, and welcomed two animals to the family: "Umi" (our gray fluffy kitten from a family member in Vermont, which was named after the math-learning cartoon *Team Umizoomi*) and Sadie (a dog that was rescued from the same man who was generous to sell us our home).

Over time, some of our relationships were mending. We were cordial, and I intentionally went out of my way to hug family at gatherings. It was very difficult for me to risk being shunned, but thankfully, I wasn't. We could handle small talk, but we still didn't feel entirely welcome. My blood comes from their blood, no matter what. Like it or not, we are family. All in all, I think everyone tries to tolerate and love one another as we worked on forgiveness. It's progress, not perfection.

I remember as we were planning Memere's eightieth birthday, I had a bad feeling that someone in our family was going to die. I didn't know who. I pleaded with God and asked Him not to allow it to happen, at least until *after* Memere's birthday party.

It's always a gamble when you plan an outdoor event with a lot of people that it might get rained out. The day was heavenly. The sun was shining on a hot July afternoon. I was fortunate to recruit some talented musicians and put a decent song list together. Mainly the old country music that my Memere likes. A couple guys from my church family joined us. Mike played bass, and Evans strummed acoustic guitar. Cousin Ray was a talented drummer. Herb chased around the babies so I could contribute. I know how difficult it was, but I was enjoying the break. I sang many a duet with my cousin Erika. Over the years as she matured, she really developed her own style. I loved it when we would sing together. It wasn't often enough. Her brother Dustin joined in as well. He dedicated "Hey Good Lookin'" to Memere while wearing a frilly apron and pot holders. He also has an amazing voice. He was strumming a guitar that our Pepere Red gave to me before he died. He made me promise he would give it to me as long as it didn't collect dust. I tried to learn and went to lessons, but I wasn't patient enough. I felt guilty because I wasn't honoring my promise. So I passed it on to Erika, and I was so glad I did! She learned some, and Dustin was able to play well too. I know Pepere Red would have been proud. It was so good to share with our relatives the gift they gave to us. Growing up, our family has always had get-togethers where they would just jam. Call it whatever you want—a gathering, shindig, or a hootenanny. My Memere would sing and harmonize with her sister Aunt Anita, and my grandfather would strum the guitar and sing some Hank Williams. My uncle Mark would join in with his guitar, and the rest of my family would join in sync with their voices. Many times it brought on emotion and caused someone to cry. I valued music. It was an intimate connection directly to the soul. It brought people together. And if you had the gift, the family loved to hear it. They would ask you to break out in song almost anytime and anywhere. As bashful I was and how awkward I felt, I loved it!

After the event was done and everyone was packing up, my uncle Mark (who almost never gets sappy) expressed his appreciation to me for doing such a great job. He praised us and asked me to make sure I told the church guys and the others how sincerely thankful he was and what a great job they did. I paused, smiled, and reassured him that I would pass it on.

I know this is unbelievable, but I have pictures of some of my family members sitting outside under the weeping willow tree at Herb's mom and dad's house *before* it belonged to them. The house used to belong to Herb's uncle's parents years ago, and they would have these gatherings with music. And do you remember the three-bay garage I describe in the beginning of the first chapter? I also have pictures when there was no rubber roof; it was a massive barn! Coincidence? I think not.

If you find that hard to believe, let me add another incredible discovery. When I was a young girl, roughly seven or so, I lived in Worcester on Plane Street. Herb lived just a few blocks away from me. We were less than a mile from each other! It makes me wonder if we ever passed by each other.

July 31, 2015 (just a little over a couple of weeks after my Memere's eightieth birthday party), smacked us upside the head, more like sucker-punched us. Even though I felt like someone was going to die, I just didn't see this one coming! My uncle Mark went to work that morning as usual. After noticing severe symptoms, he was rushed by ambulance to the hospital. He suffered an aortic dissection. It was a tumultuous couple of weeks. We added him to the prayer chains and called on Pastor Ron a few times to come to the hospital and pray with our family. It was horrible! Poor Denise slept at the hospital every night on the waiting room floor on a blow-up mattress. It was chaos at its worst. One day we had hope he was going to pull through, and other moments hope would take a nose-dive. I remember convincing Herb's mom to go to the restaurant near the hospital to take a break and get a bite to eat with me and

Herb. She worked in hospice, so she could see signs of death earlier than most would admit, including myself. I couldn't accept that God was going to take him. Fifties is still young, in my opinion. I got angry with her because I felt like she was giving up on him. But she could read between the lines. She is by far the strongest, most graceful woman I've ever known. She called for a large family gathering at the hospital and had the doctors explain in full detail what my uncle's chances were to survive and what quality of life there might be if they kept him on life support. Everyone knew how strongly my uncle felt. She unselfishly waited for a unanimous agreement before any final decisions were made. Everyone was allowed access to say their final goodbyes. It took great patience and courage for her to consider so many during a time where all was on the line. It's one thing to sign someone's health-care proxy; it's a whole other thing to actually become one. I remember having to make the heartbreaking call to one of his sons who lived out of state. That's a phone call you never want to make.

August 15, 2015, my uncle Mark took his last breath and entered past heaven's gates. How many times does my family have to go through trauma? I know death is inevitable, but why is it we can't grow old to the end? Herb's mom was widowed again! They were married for eighteen years. She was shattered, and we were crushed. How do you grieve with three small boys? How do we tell them their Puppa is gone? I'd be lying if I told you I wasn't mad at God. He disappointed me. He disappointed everybody. How could He let this happen twice? It didn't make sense. It certainly wasn't fair. Uncle Mark was only fifty-four years old. He just had a routine physical; everything was fine!

How do you comfort anyone else? We were runners by nature, flighty when times were unbearable. But we felt stuck. We had to focus on our children and our responsibilities. It was like we were reliving Herb's dad all over again. All the pain we tried to suppress from the first death wasn't going away. Even though it was tempting, we refused to drink away our problems like we did the first time. We turned to Jesus. Certain things would trigger anxiety. It was hard not to allow negative thoughts to take over. We felt on edge. We couldn't handle loud noises. We were startled easily. Herb and I were often impatient and irritable with each other. Heart palpitations and body sweats took place, and much of the time, we just didn't feel well.

The first thing Herb did was try to fix things. He usually steps in and takes charge. There was no life insurance (which is irresponsible, if you ask me if you can afford it). To leave a spouse with all the financial burden is unfair. It's hard enough grieving the loss of your loved one, but to leave that person scrambling for a way to provide for the funeral expenses and manage the bills is cruel. Herb's mom wasn't able to support herself. We talked it over and agreed to offer for his mom to come live with us again. It wasn't an easy decision, but we felt it was the right choice. You have to remember, with the exception of moving to the trailer the first and second time, we've always lived with others, or they've moved in with us. Being the oldest son, it was an unspoken expectation. Even though Herb's brothers did offer, it probably wouldn't have worked out very well. We rearranged the boys' rooms. Little Herbie would have to share a room with Ben. (He hated sharing a room. We promised him when we moved out of the trailer, he could finally have his own room again.) I felt bad about that, but what were we supposed to do? Everything was happening so fast. Our life was being rearranged and tipped upside down. Love is a sacrifice, and we wanted to make this transition as positive as possible, especially for the boys' sake.

Everyone has their own method to grieving. For me, I need time alone (a lot) to think, reflect, and cry. Music is another key element that helps. But I didn't want to reinjure Herb's mom by listening to the stuff my uncle loved, even though it would have been a blessing to me. It was much more difficult to grieve with three children and Herb's mom living with us. I didn't want to provoke her to tears, and I didn't want to cause her additional pain. I held in my hurt a lot. God has given me the gift of compassion, which isn't a gift at all. I guess you could label me an "empath." My mom had the same gift as far back as I could remember. There were no spiritual or emotional boundaries. If someone suffered, she was the one to go to. She would take on your pain as if she was experiencing it with you. She would put herself in their shoes. She could express in great detail her emotions with that person and bring some sense of consolation, even if it tore her apart. I had a keen sense of Herb's mom's emotions. I was highly sensitive and could feel what she felt at times. It was so painful. I felt sad for her, and other times I got angry at the situation she was put in. Intuitively, I could point out if she was improving or getting worse. I could read her by observing her behaviors and body language. The depth of pain could be seen if I looked into her dark-brown eyes. She couldn't hide or pretend with me; I just "knew." Some days I was literally drained from absorbing her despair and being overstimulated. Joy was being sucked from my being, and I struggled to replenish it.

I felt like I needed to be strong and keep balance in the home. I didn't want the boys to be overtaken by sorrow or depression. I wanted them to still see life through the eyes of a child. I became defensive and soon closed off my husband. When we would embrace each other, we would abruptly let go if we heard his mom come into the room out of consideration to "protect" her feelings. When she lost her husband, I lost mine in some ways. I felt guilty when Herb would lean in to kiss me goodbye before he headed out for work. The distance gradually became lengthier over time. Once, we actually were standing in the kitchen hugging each other and were so startled by his mom we pushed each other away like we were teenagers getting caught red-handed! Herb got angry and said, "Kristi, we're married. We're not doing anything wrong!" And even though he was right, I couldn't allow our display of affection. It made me feel awkward. We shouldn't have allowed this behavior to go on so long. It took years before we realized the damage we were causing to ourselves and our boys. While we were attempting to spare his mom, we were hurting ourselves. Almost two years went by before we realized our small children were not witnessing the beauty of love between a husband and a wife. They were denied the important example of physical touch between mom and dad. Again I felt like we were failing. Resentment was beginning to take up root.

I went to a women's faith conference in search for encouragement. I was able to convince my girlfriends Tina and Emma from high school to join me. There were many women from my church who attended. When the session was over, it left me with more questions. I struggled with why God allowed this to happen to our family. I felt spiritually manipulated. Maybe Uncle Mark died because my faith wasn't strong enough. Maybe my prayers were ignored. Then I realized how narcissistic that thought was. My faith was weak. After hearing many pastors on television programming, I couldn't wrap my brain around some of the things that were being taught. I couldn't decipher truth from lies.

As crowds of women were exiting the building, I stood near the stairwell and spoke with a woman from my church. I got emotional and asked Sally Anne, "Did God take my uncle because I had a lack of faith?" I believed God would heal and restore him. I thought he was going to pull through. She spoke to me so tenderly and calmed my heart. She brought me to Hebrews 5:7 NLT: "While Jesus was here on earth, he offered prayers and pleadings, with a loud cry and tears, to the one who could deliver him out of death. And God heard his prayers because of his reverence for God." Sally Anne explained to me that Jesus had perfect faith and was still denied His request. So if Jesus had perfect faith and His prayers were heard but still denied, it certainly wasn't because Jesus lacked faith that His prayers were not granted. God heard my cries; He heard my prayers. But ultimately, it is His will that prevailed, not mine. I was so thankful for the wisdom of a sister in Christ who took me aside and pointed out truth to me. It wasn't my fault. It was the will of the Father. Period. That was a lot easier for me to accept.

Our Mini Mansion

There is more than enough room in my Father's home. If this were not so, would I have told you that I am going to prepare a place for you? When everything is ready, I will come and get you, so that you will always be with me where I am.

—John 14:2–3 NLT

Autumn was upon us. The leaves were turning shades of crimson and rust. Living in the forest during the fall was breathtaking, literally! Our oldest son, Little Herbie, was playing outside with Ben raking leaves into a pile and repeatedly jumping and diving into them. I was in the house peeking out my window periodically between washing the dishes and taking care of Joey. I noticed Little Herbie stumbling to make it to the back door. At first, I thought he was just being silly; but when I opened the door for him, he could barely say the words, "Mom, I can't breathe."

Here we go again! I had already been through this multiple times with our boys, and there's nothing more terrifying than when your children can't take a breath! I called the pediatrician's office and booked an emergency appointment. We had a pulse oximeter on hand, and it was reading a lower than usual number below the 90s (upper 90s to 100 is ideal). When I brought him to the doctor's office, they immediately checked him and saw that he was wheezing, had shortness of breath, and the skin around his ribs were sucking in as he gasped for air. They quickly called for an ambulance, and we took a trip to UMass in Worcester.

I wish I could say the boys' pediatrician diagnosed them with asthma from the get-go. Even though I loved their doctor, I felt her approach wasn't proactive. We needed help to find solutions for preventative measures. How many times did our boys have to be on steroids for an asthma attack? I was able to find a pulmonologist out in Springfield who listened to my concerns. He put my mind at ease. He showed me how to treat my boys *before* an attack occurred, not just after.

I'm not a huge fan of prescription medications, but I prefer a low daily dosage inhaler of steroids than watching my child struggle to breathe. A rescue inhaler wasn't cutting it. In a perfect world, I would ask for healing, and trust me, I have. While I wait for that prayer to be answered, I'll just be thankful for the medical solution.

I did more research and learned babies that were born via Cesarean section were more likely to develop asthma-related issues. How bizarre! For some reason, Little Herbie and Joey were diagnosed with asthma; Benjamin was spared. Yet when he was a baby in his crib, I had to rush him to the emergency room for low oxygen levels too. All three of our children have been in the back of an ambulance (some more than once) for respiratory problems. I have spent many overnights in the hospital beside one child or another for their breathing. Trying not to fall asleep while holding their nebulizer mask up to their faces so they could inhale the medicinal mist put me in surrender mode. I've cried so many times in sheer exhaustion and fear for the loss of their lives. When a child goes limp in your arms and dad has to pass people with his flashing lights driving on Route 20 to get to the hospital, it gets intense. Most times it's sudden, so without notice, in a panic, we pack up the whole family like we are buggin' out!

Forget it when people are sick around them. You're freaking out because when others just get a cold, yours lands in the ER. You try to shield them from germs as best as you can. But many parents send their kids to school sick. They give 'em a shot of Children's Tylenol, slap on their backpacks, and send them off to school for the day, not realizing their decision impacts many, while their child is contagious and most likely spreading a virus or a bug to other classmates. And so the cycle begins. It's so frustrating! Then you get the unsympathetic mom who boasts of her children who never get sick. The audacity of some people! They are full of solutions and remedies (which I probably tried hundreds of times, to no avail) on how you can do a better job as a parent. Nothing fires me up more than hearing someone say, "Your kids are *always* sick!" like it's my fault or that maybe I'm neglectful in some way.

I constantly try to maintain a clean home by wiping baseboards near their beds to minimize dust, and I invest into essential oils to practice aromatherapy in hopes to boost immunity. We give our children a daily dose of probiotics and vitamins. You will never see someone smoking in our house. I do my due diligence. I repeat myself like a broken record. Every day I command our boys to wash their hands as soon as we pick them up from school. And if it's cold and flu season, I'm like a drill sergeant and require them to change their clothes after school. Yes, I even pray that God will clean our home from sickness or spiritual entities that attempt to come in and harass us (demons can have that capability). I consider myself pretty thorough. I spend extra money on organic and natural foods to avoid GMOs, pesticides, and antibiotics from putting added toxins in their little bodies. I make home-cooked meals regularly. No, I'm not perfect. You'll catch a cardboard pizza box in my trash can from time to time. And yes, I do allow our boys the occasional candy bars or ice-cream cone. But when I tell you we go through all lengths to ensure wellness, we really do.

There were perks to Mimi moving in! She offered to watch the boys every Friday night for us so we could have regular date nights to look forward to. Woo-hoo! What a gift! We were so thankful for her faithfulness. We were used to paying for babysitters regularly. God bless our babysitters! They came to our rescue and offered us reprieve a few hours a week. They were my heroes! As much as we looked forward to Fridays, so did the boys. Mimi would spoil them with treats and sometimes take them shopping for a toy or bring them through the famous drive-through for a happy meal.

Herb and his crew finally completed another house renovation in North Brookfield. They did a magnificent job! This house was huge! We were inspired to paint it salmon red with beige trim from an estate we admired on the back roads in Warren. It was originally built in 1875. This house was spacious, over 3,700 square feet! It had eight bedrooms, two front porches, and three floors! The large kitchen had custom cabinets, a wine rack, decorative shelving, and recessed lighting. The sunlight poured through the narrow-paned Victorian glass windows on the front of the home. Ceilings were high. Some of the original wooden wide-planked floors were salvaged and refurbished. It had a cute backyard (under an acre) and a two-car garage in the rear. It was around the holidays when my honey dropped me off so I could clean the house to prepare it for being listed on the market.

We were preparing it for an open house. I put up a white artificial Christmas tree and decorated it beautifully. I set it in the front window on top of the custom bench the carpenter installed. I can remember feeling unworthy of the home. It reminded me of the houses I used to clean when I worked for a cleaning business years ago. I used to study the homes' architecture and color schemes in hopes one day I would live in a fine house. Wealthy homes had some of the most intricate characteristics, unusual colors, and wallpaper prints. I loved the beauty their interior designers created in these ritzy estates. As I was cleaning and getting this house ready, I privately prayed that if God wanted our family to move again, He would allow us to keep this one for ourselves.

The house was on the market exactly ninety-one days. Surprisingly, no one scoffed it up. It wasn't making much sense to me—beautiful home, nice neighborhood, reasonable price, and completely restored. Then Herb asked me if I wanted the house. I remember getting the feeling of butterflies in my belly. I didn't want to manipulate him to give our family this house when we really needed to sell it for income, but he told me he knew I loved the house; and now that his mom moved in, we could use the extra space and privacy. Yes, I cried again, when he placed the small nickel-plated brass key to the house in the palm of my hand! The boys ran through the entire house like it was Christmas morning. They loved how gigantic it was. The place echoed! I thought to myself, there was no way we would have enough furniture to ever fill it!

There was only one problem: the stairs. They were steep, and there were a lot of steps. I was very nervous that the boys might trip or fall down on them. They made me nervous. Herb agreed to install a carpet so at least the landing would be soft, if, in fact, that was ever to happen.

How exciting! What a way to bring in the new year! It was refreshing and new for all of us. Mimi would have her own spacious bedroom downstairs, and the boys could have their pick from the rooms on the second floor. Third floor was out of the question; I wasn't running up two flights of stairs to play referee! Maybe when they got a little older. It didn't take long to accumulate much. We painted the boys' rooms again the colors they chose and counted our blessings for our new older home.

I used to call it our mini mansion. That's what it felt like to me. God gives good gifts. When we get up to heaven, I doubt God will assign us a shack for the rest of our forever lives. He promises us an eternal dwelling place with Him. Maybe a house with many rooms will be like a mansion. One day we will find out! "No eye has seen, no ear has heard, and no mind has imagined what God has prepared for those who love him" (1 Corinthians 2:9 NLT).

Herb really catered to me. He was tired of moving every couple of years and wanted us to finally settle, especially for the boys' sake. We were thankful the boys had school choice, and we were able to keep them in the same elementary school. We loved their school. The boys were familiar with their friends and teachers; it just wouldn't feel right to pull them out and put them in different schools. Even though kids are resilient, it was very important to us to provide consistency, especially with all the times we relocated.

I'm no expert, but you probably shouldn't transplant fruit trees in January when you live in Massachusetts. My honey was tired of losing the fruit to his hard labor. So on an unusually warm muddy day in January, he and a buddy dug a hole as I prayed and hoped our dwarf apple tree and peach tree would survive.

I dare not complain, but with more square footage, I was constantly trying to keep this palace clean! More rooms for the boys to make their messes—there were three of them and only one of me! I was outnumbered. I really did feel cherished by my honey. He went out of his way and gave me a huge walk-in closet right in the laundry quarters. I now had a neat, tidy, and organized shelving system for all of our clothes and shoes.

Uncle Sam and Auntie "Manda" came down from Vermont to visit (they're not really the kids' aunt and uncle, but they were deserving of the title). Auntie made homemade old-fashioned doughnuts with the boys, and we convinced Uncle Sam that we weren't going to move again; that was the only way he would agree to help us hang the tire swing on the tree in the back behind the house. Their youngest of three, Alleigh, loved to come visit the boys (she is the basketball guru in the family). She would spend quality time with them and keep them occupied while we attempted to have conversation as adults.

God definitely had His hand in on all the details. There was a younger couple we cared about from our church. We'll call them Tate and Hannah. The husband, Tate, used to work for Herb when he had his plumbing business. They moved into the trailer park around the time we lived there, and I can remember talking to the wife, Hannah, about her hopes to eventually move out and find a home of their own. She and I got along quite well. They were becoming more independent and learning the ropes to marriage, kids, and adulting. She told me that she and her husband went to look at the house in Warren before we became owners. She told me that they were interested in the house for themselves, and when they went to take a look at it, she got stung on the deck by some wasps.

I asked Herb if he would consider selling the house to them even though they may not have the ability to go for a mortgage right away. He said he would ask Tate if he was even interested. After communicating to Tate, my husband could tell he was interested but reluctant to pursue or explore options. He was a conservative guy. I nudged my honey to surprise them and tell them they could pay us rent until a bank would grant them a mortgage, and that we would be willing to do a rent-to-own situation. Why not? We were blessed with grace in that exact home by a guy who gave us two years to refinance. Why not pay it forward?

That was one of the best phone calls we ever made! I remember Herb calling Tate and telling him to have his wife come near the phone. Herb spoke loudly, "The house is yours!" They didn't understand what we were proposing. We told them if they really loved the house and wanted it, we would work something out so that they could have it. We mutually came to the agreement that they would use their trailer at the park as a deposit for the purchase of the home, and the remainder balance would be a loan until they could find financing. They were so happy and excited. I know in my heart that house was meant for them. Even though we all went out on a limb, the bank did, in fact, approve them to purchase the house anyway! It was a win-win! On the rare occasion I bump into Hannah, she still makes it a point to compliment their home. They seem appreciative after all these years, and we got to witness their beautiful family grow. It takes great faith to risk moments like that one, but there's no better feeling than being able to bless others.

> Here's my point. A stingy sower will reap a meager harvest, but the one who sows from a generous spirit will reap an abundant harvest. Let giving flow from your heart, not from a sense of religious duty. Let it spring up freely from the joy of giving-all because God loves hilarious generosity. Yes, God is more than ready to overwhelm you with every form of grace, so that you will have more than enough of everything—every moment and in every way. He will make you overflow with abundance in every good thing you do. (2 Corinthians 9:6–8 The Passion Translation)

Remember those bear drills? Shortly after we moved out, Herb got a call from our old neighbor to take a swing by and see what he hunted close to our back woods. He had a gigantic black bear hanging from a tree on the front of his property. It must have been eight to nine feet tall, without exaggeration. His sharp claws were intimidating. Our boys were stunned and in awe. They had never seen anything quite like this before, especially this close! This beast was unfathomable! All I could say was, "I told you so!" I think if I saw that animal prowling around my backyard, I would have freaked out!

We had a lot of sweet memories at our mini mansion. Herb's Auntie Judy and his brother Keith asked us to get baptized in our inexpensive Intex aboveground pool. Keith has been baptized a handful of times (even though one time is sufficient); he felt the need to rededicate himself again.

Maybe you're wondering, how is it that *you* were able to baptize? (Technically, I didn't; it was my honey.) I know a lot of people assume you have to be baptized by a priest or a pastor. Different churches have different requirements. Let me share with you what Jesus said: "Therefore, go and make disciples of all the nations, baptizing them in the name of the Father and the Son and the Holy Spirit" (Matthew 28:19 NLT). I'm pretty sure Jesus wasn't referring to just the twelve disciples. First Peter 2:5 NLT says, "And you are living stones that God is building into his spiritual temple. What's more, *you are his holy priests.* Through the mediation of Jesus Christ, you offer spiritual sacrifices that please God."

What do you do when your child says to you, "Mom, I want to be baptized"? Do you wait and schedule the baptism with your local pastor? Do you deny him? Do you make the child wait till he or she gets older? Jesus said, "Let the little children come to me and do not hinder them, for the kingdom of heaven belongs to such as these" (Matthew 19:14 NIV). Joey was taking a bath one night, and out of the clear blue, he asked if he could be baptized! It was just four days after his fourth birthday. What was I to say? "No, son, you're too young. You don't really understand what you're asking me to do." While I did delay for a moment, I told him, "Yes, let me get your daddy." And so Joey was baptized that day. We asked him if he wanted to make Jesus his Lord and if he wanted Jesus to save him. We also asked him if he wanted to go to heaven one day. You improvise as best as you can. Who am I to question if his heart is sincere or not? Matthew 18:3 NLT says, "I tell you the truth, unless you turn from your sins and become like little children, you will never get into the Kingdom of Heaven."

I mean no disrespect, but I'm a simple person. If God puts it on your heart to share the Gospel or to follow through with baptizing someone, and if He gives you the ability, then be obedient. We had a great teacher; we witnessed Pastor Ron baptize dozens of people of all ages. We don't take the opportunity lightly; we consider it a privilege when someone asks to be baptized. We never want to discourage anyone from the calling of God. Even John the Baptist (Jesus's cousin) considered himself unworthy of baptizing Jesus.

> Then Jesus went from Galilee to the Jordan River to be baptized by John. But John tried to talk him out of it. "I am the one who needs to be baptized by you," he said, "so why are you coming to me?" but Jesus said, "It should be done, for we must carry out all that God requires." So, John agreed to baptize him. (Matthew 3:13–15 NLT)

From time to time, we would talk about Jesus with our boys and extend the invitation openly. Ben seemed scared to make that decision when we approached him. We didn't pressure him, manipulate him, or embarrass him. We told him when he was ready, he would know, and it was okay. We reassured him that we still loved him and that Jesus did too. Months later during vacation, he told us that he was ready. He was confident from swimming in the pool that he would be able to pinch his nose and actually be safe for the split second he was being submerged.

Little Herbie made the decision early on as well; he chose to have Pastor Ron and his dad baptize him at Lake Lashaway with our church family. Mimi, Auntie Windy (Keith's wife), and Katrina (our niece) were also baptized that day.

What does baptism signify? My basic definition would be this: it is an outward display of what has already taken place internally in the heart when someone commits their life to Jesus Christ. The old is dead with Christ (crucified), and the new is born again (resurrected). It is a representation of our soul being washed clean and forgiven. It's a demonstration of showing the world around us that we boldly proclaim we belong to Jesus. It's a celebration of being adopted by God!

I can remember Herb and I attending a picnic after a church service at a private home owned by a sweet older couple from our church. They had a beautiful pond behind their home and invited everyone who wanted to come. I wore a coral suit and had no plans whatsoever to be baptized. Pastor Ron refused to accept my refusal. He insisted that I was getting baptized that afternoon. I didn't bring a change of clothes and was very uncomfortable being dunked in front of so many people. Truthfully, I felt God nudging me to be obedient. After my honey was baptized by Pastor Ron and Patrick, I willingly trudged through the cold murky water (suit and all) and was moved by the experience of having my body submerged under the water and coming up feeling a newness. It was a beautiful experience. I'm so pleased for following through with my compulsive decision and the coercion of our pastor.

One of the most urgent baptisms I have ever witnessed was when Erika called me up one night and told me she was so desperate to get baptized she didn't care if she found a puddle! Often she was spontaneous! As adamant as she was, I was able to convince her not to plunge herself that cold and dark winter night. I warned her that she'd probably end up with hypothermia and suggested for her to just come over in the morning. It was around 7:30 a.m. when she called me. She was parked in our driveway, eager to get dunked! Our uncle Kevin came with her to show support and take part in the celebration. So before the kids went off to school, Herb took out his Bible, and Uncle Kevin prayed as she was immersed in our Jacuzzi tub. It was another heartwarming and joyous moment.

When you make the decision to surrender to Jesus Christ and make Him the Lord of your life, it is an act of free will. You cannot force anyone to become saved, including infants. That is why we believe in dedicating our children to the Lord. The difference between dedication and baptizing is significant. When we dedicate our children to God, we are asking for Him to hedge our child and protect them, to bless them, and to give them faith. One of the most common prayers our pastor prays is from the book of Numbers 6:24–26: "May the Lord bless you and protect you. May the Lord smile on you and be gracious to you. May the Lord show you his favor and give you his peace." That's one of my favorites! We ask as parents and stewards of that child that God would intervene on their behalf and ultimately that their names be written in the Lamb's book of life—that they would be sensitive to God's calling on their lives and eventually make the eternal decision for *themselves* to accept Jesus Christ as their personal Lord and Savior. It's not a religious ceremony that assumes, because the child has been sprinkled with holy water, they are forever saved. That can be very misleading and confusing in my opinion.

Herb and I never like to be stuck without options. We appreciate oil heat, but both agree there should be a secondary way to supply heat in our home. One time we lost electricity for almost a full week in the winter during a nasty ice storm when I was pregnant with Little Herbie, and while many of our neighbors had to relocate and their pipes froze, we were able to stay in our home and help others because we had a woodstove. My honey found a great deal at a local hardware store and bought the floor model for our mini mansion. He designed a brick archway in our dining room so we could install a similar woodstove like the one we used to have. I was enamored by the complexity of the workmanship that his carpenter crafted. His crew was very talented. We had a single brick etched by another skilled man with the word *Bethel* on it. It means "house of God." Mimi and Auntie Judy painstakingly wallpapered the tall walls in the family room of an elegant vintage rose pattern with a black printed background. We were making it ours, personalizing it with our own uniqueness. The boys helped paint the flagpole, and our carpenter friend was daring enough to string up our American flag. He climbed a thirty-foot ladder that rested on nothing more than the pole itself. He threaded the rope through the top of the pole, quite a noble and daring task. We were contemplating calling the fire department to see if they would be willing to help us out; that certainly would have been the safer route. The dwarf apple tree produced leaves but did not produce apples yet; we were just grateful it survived.

My friend from high school Emma inspired me to buy a large inflatable jumpy house for the boys. When I went to visit her, she had a huge princess castle in her bedroom for her two younger daughters. As she plugged it in, the air filled up this heavy-duty nylon material. It was an instant play place for the girls! What a fantastic idea, especially for the colder months, when the kids don't get a lot of play-time outdoors. I stole her idea and surprised the boys with their own jumpy house I found at a discounted price. They were superthrilled when they saw the built-in basketball hoop and got to go down the slide. We had plenty of room now that we had the entire third floor.

In defiance, my honey built the boys an impressive tree house. We were supposed to close on a house we had for sale in Brookfield. It fell through on closing day for some minor technicality. The bank pulled financing on the clients that were purchasing our property. We were so angry because we waited three months to get paid, and we were planning on taking a family vacation down South to see Auntie Keri (we only see her a couple times a year). We felt bad for the people who wanted the home too; how devastated they must have felt! So on the boys' school vacation we, had the crew come and put their talents to magic. If you ask me, the grown-ups were sentimental. Patrick was reminiscing his childhood years as he was building this expensive fort. We hauled in sand for the lower section of the massive sandbox. Dad found a slide on the side of the road that someone was giving away, so he attached that to the top decking. The landing went into another smaller sandbox to offer cushion for their behinds. The trunk of the red maple tree was centered perfectly inside. It had two windows and a screen door off the front porch. We used wooden shingles for the roof and added a rope swing. We didn't have cash, but we had credit we could rack up. The expense was a response out of impulse and emotion: a reaction to the unforeseen cancellation to a sale.

As for those steep mountain stairs in our mini mansion? Little Herbie had a terrifying nightmare one night and woke up Dad by standing over him in the dark by his side of the bed. Not only was Dad startled from Little Herbie, but Dad's reaction freaked out our son. They scared each other. We tried to console our son and reassure him. I was in such a hurry I didn't turn the hallway lights on. I went downstairs to grab something, not realizing Umi (our cat) was lounging on the second step from the top of the stairs. I took a step, and as I felt something, I quickly retracted my leg in hopes of not hurting her. There I went—I slipped down the whole flight of stairs! I was thankful I didn't tumble forward and do a summersault! I skidded down on my back and derriere, hitting every railing post with my right arm on the way down. Herb wasn't the most sympathetic guy when those sorts of things happened. He was more annoyed by me falling than worried that I needed medical attention! After hearing me fall down the stairs, my knight in shining armor didn't come to my rescue. He yelled, "What was that?" In a frustrated tone, I yelled back, "I fell down the stairs! I'm okay!" (More like, Just leave me alone! I know you can't handle the drama!)

The funniest thing about Herb's mom is, she is hard of hearing. A train could have plowed through the house, and she would not have been alarmed. She had no clue it ever even happened till I shared it with her in the morning! I had ugly bruises from that fall that lasted over a week! Being a glass-half-full kind of gal, I was thankful it was me and not one of the kids. The other thought I had was, *I'm glad I got that fear over with!* I was less likely to fall again and make the same mistake twice. After that mishap, you can be sure I habitually grasped the railing tighter than usual and always flipped the light switch on when I needed to go downstairs! Thank God for Drew Hicks, my physical therapist!

Unsatisfied

"Teacher, which is the most important commandment in the law of Moses?" Jesus replied, "You must love the Lord your God with all your heart, all your soul, and all your mind. This is the first and greatest commandment. A second is equally important: Love your neighbor as yourself."

—Matthew 22:36–39 NLT

I used to hate when my honey would try to explain to others why we changed addresses again. I felt like a spoiled, difficult-to-please diva. He would say things like, "She fell in love with it," or "She just wasn't happy being at so and so" (whichever address we were in last). Even though he was right to some extent, I didn't like the way it sounded. To me, it came off as shallow, superficial, and ungrateful.

We could come up with multiple excuses to leave, but the bottom line was, I never really felt like we were home. That's why Herb always worked so hard at trying to make it our home with all the renovations. Deep down, we really wanted to have a farmhouse with animals, a barn, a good portion of clean land for gardens, and simple, affordable living. We loved the idea of privacy. Even though we had friendly neighbors, there's something awkward about sitting outside having your cup of coffee in your bathrobe feeling the obligation to wave hello, or little things like trying to discipline our wild and crazy boys knowing next door can hear my every threat. I didn't want to know their business, and we certainly didn't want them to know ours.

Now we lived half a mile up the street from my brother and his family. After way too many years, my brother tied the knot with the love of his life. I was so happy for them. They usually don't draw much attention to themselves; they are down-to-earth, humble people. They held a beautiful ceremony at a church in Leicester and celebrated their special day at the same place we had our reception many years ago. All three of our nephews looked so handsome and grown up in their formal attire, stylish fedora hats, and sunglasses. It was an autumn wedding. I treated the bride to getting her hair done by a talented friend of mine. My friend Rachael was the only one I trusted to cut my hair (for good reason). She was more than just my hairdresser and friend; she was practically my psychologist! (There's something therapeutic and relaxing being pampered in her black swivel chair.)

Kelli wasn't a fussy woman who needed to spend a lot of time getting ready. She was naturally beautiful with glowing flawless skin and auburn hair. I almost had her convinced to try false eyelashes, but that's just not her. She allowed me to do her makeup as long as I promised to keep it natural! Simplicity looked radiant on her. I can remember the time Nate wanted to propose to Kelli. I was feeling guilty of the bling I had from a purchase I made for myself at Zale's. When we were going through our financial collapse, I didn't feel right wearing the ring. The blinding cluster of diamonds might have given others the assumption we were wealthy. I couldn't wear that ring with a good conscience. I felt like a hypocrite. So I gladly offered my brother the ring in exchange for weekly payments. I paid a lot for it but offered it to him at an affordable price. We got to witness Nate traditionally get down on one knee at their kitchen table and ask Kelli if she would marry him. She smiled, extended her open arms to him, and without hesitation, accepted his proposal.

One other time, my honey and I were at a Christian bookstore in Auburn and noticed a comical sign at the front desk. It read, "Accepting donations, I want to propose to my girlfriend!" We asked the young cashier if he was serious. He told us he loved his girlfriend and wanted to truly propose to her, so we called him on it. I showed him the heirloom-quality diamond ring on my finger (it held no sentimental value). I told him it was appraised at over $2,000 and that I would sell it to him way below value. He accepted the proposition. Later, we were happy to find out she said yes!

It was so special to be part of Nate and Kelli's long-awaited and much-deserved moment. Nathan came over to the house unexpectedly with all three of our nephews the day of his wedding to ask my honey if he could help him with their ties. I snapped a couple pictures of their dapper poses (while I was still in my bathrobe, not nearly ready) on the front porch before they headed off to the church. As much as we tried to be on time, after we picked up my mom, we missed the first few moments and quietly snuck in our pews.

Auntie Kelli was a major help to us when I was promoted to mommyhood. We hired her to fill in for me and help with secretarial duties to keep our business running. There was no realistic way I was able to both meet the demands of being mom to three young'uns and manage a couple of businesses. She would come over and balance books, type out estimates, prepare billing, make phone calls, and many other tasks. I appreciated her help and looked forward to her visits. I was desperate for adult conversation and would offer her tea or a healthy shake. She generously gave more than what was required. Our clients loved her; she was very professional and had friendly customer service skills. She was gracious for taking the time to listen to my complaints. There were times she would be bombarded by not just me but the kids. They were hungry for her affection and attention just as much as I was! She often made it a point to take a few minutes to sit on the floor and play a game or put a puzzle together with the boys.

Minor changes were happening with my body. I was responding to stress in peculiar ways. At first, the symptoms were manageable and subtle. I wasn't entirely sure what was going on, but I passed things off, hoping the symptoms would eventually just disappear.

There were only a couple times as a mom I escaped overnight to recharge my batteries. Herb reassured me he could "man the fort" and give me a few days to spend some time with my sister. I struggled leaving my babies, but knew it was best that I take some time and get some much-needed rest to rejuvenate. I flew to Florida to see my twin. The first day I was there, I coma-slept. It was over twelve hours! Being a mom, that *never* happens. I'm up a couple times a night between bathroom breaks and checking on the boys. (It became a habit since the time I checked on Ben in his crib, and he couldn't breathe as a baby). Many a night, I've tiptoed in their rooms and refrained from freaking out if I didn't see a pulse. I would place my hand under their nostrils to make sure all was well. One way I can describe my full-time position as mom was by comparing it to the long hours Dad put in at work throughout his day. As soon as he comes home, he can rest a bit before the next workday. For me, each day jumps into the night, and each night goes into the day. I go 24-7. There is no break. I am constantly punched in on the clock. My guard is always up. And because my honey is a sound sleeper, I know he most likely wouldn't hear anything over his own snoring, so I'm nominated night duty too. I very rarely can turn myself off. Inevitably, I get burnt out. That's why it's so important to take a break when I'm offered the opportunity. As difficult as it is to leave my family, it's necessary and beneficial for all of us.

Bonnie posted a fantastic article that helped give me some perspective as a mom. The title was "The Days Are Long but the Years Are Short." It gave me wisdom on how to appreciate the difficult times of babies, feedings, crying, and diaper changes because one day I'm going to blink, and the nest will be empty. I didn't want to wish the hard times away. I wanted to be present in the moment that I was in. As a reminder, I wrote that phrase with a dry erase marker on my mirror in my bedroom. Each morning when I got up, I would look at that mirror and smile. That quote got me through many haggard days!

I left for five days and four nights. While I was gone, my honey loved to surprise me. He invested a good chunk of money and had his amazing crew completely remodel our upstairs. They did a spectacular job! I was so overwhelmed when I came through the door. Herb brightened the dining room with a mango-orange paint (which impressed me because he picked it out, and he is color blind!). He and the boys were so excited to point out the changes that were made since I left. It seemed impossible to complete everything that got done in just four short days. My honey decorated many of the rooms with bouquets and floral arrangements from a florist out of Spencer. When he took me upstairs, I was blown away. He created a master suite you could have seen in a *Better Homes and Gardens* magazine! The walls were a baby blue with white trim. I couldn't believe (having three small boys) he dared to have white wall-to-wall carpeting installed! He bought us a king-sized bed and a mosaic outdoor bistro set for a private space to read and drink tea. The bedding looked like a fluffy cloud of cotton! He chose a white feathered down comforter with several pillows to match. A few of them were embroidered with an eyelet pattern for texture.

Sheer white drapes covered the tall window, and a soft white sheer canopy hung from the ceiling over the four wooden posts of the bed. He even installed a teardrop glass chandelier. It looked like quarters for a princess! Another sign added to my collection reads on a white rustic background with a sunflower: "In the morning when I rise, give me Jesus!" (I love that song!) As I continued to walk through our new bedroom, I noticed he installed a private retreat master bathroom. I loved the colonial blue hues on the walls, the oversized Jacuzzi tub, and the his-and-her bathroom sinks. It was gorgeous! When I was taking the tour, we heard our cat Umi faintly meowing. Herb realized she must have crawled into the access panel to the Jacuzzi tub that day when they were rushing to get it done. Herb grabbed a crowbar and opened the panel and rescued our furry feline. We all got a good laugh and were so thankful she was okay!

And just when I thought the surprise should end, as I continued to walk through the bedroom, I was led into our family "snuggle room." I thought someday that extra space that used to be the office would make a terrific snuggle room. He bought bean-bag chairs, added a flat-screen TV, an electric fireplace, and finished off the floor with fresh carpeting. I was completely taken back and overwhelmed by all the love that he and his team poured out; I was tongue-tied. There was no way now I dared to reveal my thoughts. When I had time away with my sister, I had every intention when I returned home to ask my honey if we should sell the house and move. I wasn't about to say a word now!

One night (after we tucked the boys in), we decided to watch a movie together in our new snuggle room. We bought a movie not knowing it would inspire and influence us to make some major life-changing decisions. The title of it was *To Joey, with Love*. The documentary is about a well-known country music couple. Joey (the wife) shares the challenges of battling cancer. Rory (the husband) records much of the footage. The love they had for each other and the Lord is indescribable! They shared their story in such a vulnerable way. What I can tell you is, I wasn't the only one in tears. I've witnessed my honey cry less than a dozen times my whole life. This movie pierced him. Their faith was beyond comprehensible. By far one of the most meaningful love stories we've ever watched.

We both agreed it was time to go for the dream and take big risks. We didn't want to settle anymore. We were intentional about finding where we were meant to be. So we began to search on popular real estate sites online. We were looking for the one place we were meant to be, our home. We knew there was a small window of time we needed to find a place to plant our roots for the sake of the boys, and we just couldn't envision being in the mini mansion forever. As much as it was beautiful, if I had to grumble and complain about anything, here were my excuses for packing up: One, it was too close to the road. Two, every time the wind blew, we would smell the chemicals from the rubber factory up the street. Three, because the house was so large, it was costly to keep it warm in the colder months (which is basically nine months out of the year). Four, we wanted more land for four-wheelers, gardens, and farm animals. This one acre only allowed us a small garden and a handful of egg-laying hens. Five, which is by far one of my biggest gripes, we had to pay quarterly town water and sewer bills on top of our already expensive mortgage, real estate taxes, and insurance. Plus, we didn't like the idea that our family was being exposed to the treatments of chlorine in our drinking water. We are both well-water fans.

We were approaching school vacation, and on a random Sunday morning, I came across a listing in Harrodsburg, Kentucky. Spontaneously, I asked my honey if we could take a road trip to the southern state of Kentucky. He asked me, "When? Right now?" I smiled and said, "Yes, now." The boys love to go on vacation. They overheard our conversation and already had their luggage ready. So we packed up the kids and our luggage and headed down south. We couldn't convince Mimi to come. I don't think she knew what to think. By this time, she already moved twice in less than two years. Our family thrives on road trips. We love to escape life and hit the blacktop. It's fun to imagine living somewhere other than where we are. It wasn't unusual for us to fantasize about traveling the states in an RV. We've already been to Tennessee, Texas, and Florida (and all the states in between). When Little Herbie was only ten months old, we drove over thirty-eight hours to the Grand Canyon.

Speaking of road trips, that reminds me of the time we went to Texas to visit my sister. (She often moved just like we did. As long as she lived closer to the equator and had a palm tree, she was happy.) Anyway, Joey couldn't have been three months old yet. It was the kind of vacation that if something could go wrong, it did. Keri had a beautiful house near Dallas. This house was spacious and had enough room for multiple guests. The kids loved to swim in her pool. It was a highly populated area. Let me back up a bit. Before we even left, there was a severe storm headed our way. My honey recommended we cancel the trip. I suggested the alternative option: to drive "around" the storm that was coming to New England. We drove our minivan down and escaped the blizzard, but we had our own set of problems. I can remember as we were driving through Arkansas, the trees and the grass were covered in ice for miles. It was so barren I remember distinctly saying out loud, "If there is any state I wouldn't want to break down in, it is Arkansas!" We arrived safely to Auntie Keri's. She never gets snow in Texas! Of course, she blamed us Northerners for the light dusting (we must have brought it down from Massachusetts).

My sister got a distressing phone call from our cousin. I've never heard him so disturbed. He said he needed to see Keri and that he was coming down immediately. We prayed that he would arrive safely. I had a feeling this journey was appointed by God. Our cousin was having his own set of problems even finding the means of transportation. He literally took a taxi, a bus, a train, and a plane to get there! He was so disheveled when he finally arrived. You could tell his nerves were shot. He was shaking like a leaf and chain-smoking. We talked with him, and God was brought up. He had a lot of questions about our faith, and we extended the invitation to him. He didn't hesitate to pray with us and ask Jesus into his heart. The transformation was immediate! I took pictures of him before the prayer and after. His face was at peace, and he was a new man!

Herb offered to give him a haircut, and he went outside to smoke a cigar. Then he asked me the question I didn't want him to. He asked me if he had to give up his "way of life." I knew that was going to come up, but I wasn't expecting him to ask me that soon. I took out my Bible and had to explain the truth, whether he liked it or not. I read scripture with love and no condemnation. You could tell it was a stronghold for him. We all ended up spending time together that week. I really enjoyed catching up with him.

We went to the aquarium. Then as we parted our separate ways, Keri told me she wanted me to take some cash just in case. She handed me a thousand dollars. It was unusual for us to loan money to each other. All she said was, "Kristi, take it while I have it, and if someday I need it in return, you can lend me a helping hand." I appreciated her generosity and graciously accepted it.

Well, if you can believe it, our minivan broke down in Arkansas! Seriously! And we needed the thousand dollars to get it fixed! We were stranded on the side of the highway, and the police officer escorted us to the nearest hotel. All three of our boys were in their glory in the back of the cruiser. I told them that better be the first and last time they were ever in one too! We stayed at a hotel, and it took three long days till the vehicle could be repaired. What can you do with three active boys in a hotel room? Thank God, we were in walking distance to a Cracker Barrel. My honey refused to have the car worked on by the first auto mechanic—they were way too expensive—so he asked the woman at the desk of the hotel whom she recommended. She referred us to another guy. Only God can orchestrate these details!

The man who fixed our car gave us an amazing deal and even worked on our vehicle during the weekend because he knew we were trying to get back home. The mechanic got to talking with my honey and told him he recently just had a heart attack. My honey point-blank asked him if he died, did he know where he would be going? This guy explained to my honey that he and his wife used to go to church frequently but was betrayed by his wife when he found out she was cheating on him with the pastor. He told my honey he didn't know why he was telling him such personal information about himself, that he's not generally that way. Herb was able to share his testimony about how God rescued him from a terrible lawsuit and blessed us with children after ten years of infertility. The man openly gave his heart that day to Jesus Christ! How miraculous! And just when you think you've heard it all, God blew us away again!

The next day, we decided to take the boys to the McDonald's down the street. I was hoping it had a play place; it didn't. We stuck out like a sore thumb, five of us walking the side of a main road on our way back from McDonald's to our hotel. Then a woman stepped on her brakes and rolled her window down on a main road and asked us if we were the couple from Massachusetts. We were confused at how she knew about us. She said she knew someone at the hotel we were staying at and heard our story. My honey was nervous for her because it was very dangerous to stop in the middle of a busy road, so she pulled over to the side and handed us a one-hundred-dollar bill and explained that God told her to give it to us! We were in shock and thanked her.

Another woman pulled her car around behind her. She said, "I never do this kind of stuff, but God wanted you to have this." She handed us a twenty-dollar bill. As humbling as it was for us to receive money from strangers, I was so encouraged at a time when I felt so abandoned and discouraged. We obviously were not there by chance. We ended up breaking down one last time in Tennessee, but eventually we did make it back home, and guess how much money it took for us to get there? You guessed it—$120.00 between fuel and food! We needed a vacation from our vacation!

I love holding my honey hostage and going on adventures together with my family. We navigated through the eastern states and finally reached our destination. The kind realtor showed us around the place. It had a lot of potential: eighteen acres with a couple barns and outbuildings, large oak trees, a brook, beautiful landscapes, and a farmhouse I could envision our family in. It needed a bit of work. It was a fixer-upper, but the price was reasonable. I was ready to make a drastic change. My thought was, *What do we have to lose?* Worst-case scenario: if we hate it, we can always move back up to Massachusetts and say we tried. I figured family could come and visit for weeks at a time, and Mimi already made it clear she'd follow us no matter where we went. We asked the realtor for her business card, and I was already scheming ways on how I was going to convince my honey on taking the plunge! I figured we had a fourteen-hour drive; might as well put that time to good use.

Right as we were merging onto the highway on Route 64 east, we saw the strangest thing! There was an old lady (in her seventies) on the ramp toward the highway with a backpack, wearing a baseball cap carrying a couple of bags in ninety-degree weather. She approached our truck, and as soon as I rolled down my window to see if she was okay, she asked us for a ride to Virginia! I glared at my honey like, *You better not!* But before we could give her an answer, I was climbing in the back with our three boys while she hitched a ride shotgun! What were we going to say? "No, ma'am, sorry we can't help you." I felt bad for her. What in the world was she doing all alone on the highway? Why was she headed to Virginia? What did she have in that backpack? So as she sat on my cell phone, I thought, *I hope I don't need to call 911 because I'm not grabbing it under her leg!* I did what I always do—I prayed! I prayed she wasn't mentally ill or deranged and intending on harming my hubby or us in the back seat. She seemed nice. She was wearing a long-sleeve denim shirt, pants, and sneakers. Herb made small conversation with her to pass the time. She didn't really include me in on the conversation. I tried a couple of times to rescue my honey; that didn't work very well. He was on his own. Now I felt like the hostage!

The boys, who are usually loud and noisy, were exceptionally quiet. I could tell they felt uncomfortable; all three of them were clinging to me. I tried to listen as best as I could to her conversation, but it was difficult because the windows were rolled down. She was an odd duck. She sounded much like a conspiracy theorist. She was saying some of the most outlandish things. Not that we told her we were hunting for a home, but she went on to tell us all the reasons we didn't want to move to Kentucky. She had moved there over forty years ago and worked with horses. She explained to us the caterpillars down there were causing great problems with the horses, sometimes even death, and the horses she worked with were expensive thoroughbreds. She also mentioned that she has severe asthma, and her doctor suggested she moved. Then she told us that you never want to move to Kentucky because there's a stockpile of chemical weapons being kept there since the 1940s that they've been trying to get moved for years.

Another thing she warned us about was that there was a pastor who was wanted for murder and how you can't tell the wolves from the sheep. To top it off, she went on to say the Ku Klux Klan (a hateful white-supremacist group) is still very much active in that area. That can't be! She must be off her rocker! I couldn't wait for her to leave. Herb asked her if she had any money, and of course, she said no. He knew the only way to get rid of her was to get her a hotel. I think she would have adopted us and moved in with us permanently! We patiently endured through an hour and a half with this strange stranger. Herb noticed that next to the gas station was a hotel. He went in with the woman and dug out some cash from his wallet so she could safely stay the night. And that was the last time we ever saw her.

Boy, were my plans destroyed! I googled everything she said, and the crazy thing was, she was spot on! Who was this woman? We took it as a sign that we were not meant to move to Kentucky. Was this person an angel? I really can't say; I guess it's possible! Hebrews 13:2 says, "Don't forget to show hospitality to strangers, for some who have done this have entertained angels without realizing it!"

Chasing Rainbows

Look here, you who say, "Today or tomorrow we are going to a certain town and will stay there a year. We will do business there and make a profit." How do you know what your life will be like tomorrow? Your life is like the morning fog—it's here a little while, then it's gone. What you ought to say is, "If the Lord wants us to, we will live and do this or that." Otherwise you are boasting about your own pretentious plans, and all such boasting is evil.

—James 4:13–16 NLT

When we first became *Christians* (followers of Jesus Christ), I was so fascinated when God revealed the meaning of why He created rainbows. It was a promise to Noah that he would never flood the entire earth again. I suppose, if I was Noah, I probably would have appreciated that promise, considering he and his family were the only human survivors of the world's most catastrophic flood. Who would want to go through that twice?

I was kind of bummed out that Kentucky was out of the question. My honey told me he did find something along the lines of what we were looking for on Zillow in Warren. Even though it wasn't the location I desired, I was willing to check it out. As soon as my honey pulled up the listing, my heart skipped a beat! I asked him how long it was on the market for, and he told me that he noticed the listing the same time we saw the one in Kentucky. It's rare to find the old farmhouse with outbuildings, a barn, a body of water, and land. Most of them are passed down to generations of families or sold off at auctions. And they can be pricey. I couldn't believe he didn't tell me about this one sooner. I was feening! It was everything we wanted! It was too good to be true. It had thirty-five acres, two ponds, stone-walled borders, and the farmhouse was built in the 1800s. I couldn't believe my eyes! It also had a massive barn, fruit trees, and the most heavenly view of the mountains. The mighty oak tree in the front was majestic, the trunk bragging the glory of being centuries old. I needed to see it right away! So we took a ride as a family, and I didn't even need to step foot in the house—I wanted this place! It reminded me of the similar landscape I grew up with as a kid. Across the street was a dairy farm. The cows were grazing in the pasture. This had to be *the one*! My honey pulled in and spoke with the owner and told him that we were interested in the house.

I was beyond elated; I was emotional. I couldn't believe there was such a place in our state! We pursued our options very aggressively; nothing was stopping us! We quickly put our mini mansion on the market and prayed hard that we would sell it quickly. The owner to the farmhouse accepted our offer, but it was contingent on us being able to sell ours. We were ecstatic! We would muster up any excuse just to get permission to go on the premises. We took our boys there and pulled out the tape measures and began designing an addition for Herb's mom. Sometimes we would park up on the hill and admire the view. We were so confident we even began introducing ourselves to some of the neighbors. We informed them that we were in the process of buying the property. I don't know why we were both so restless; it was a combination of excitement and fear at the same time. What if our house didn't sell? What if we had a hard time getting a mortgage? What if the boys were too young to respect the ponds? If we ever had any doubt, I liked to run our ideas by Harold and Jane Harper. They gave us the pros and cons and tried to keep our heads out of the clouds. We respected them and trusted their advice, even though we didn't always follow it. (A sister in Christ used to tell me, "Do you think humankind would still be here if Noah followed advice from others?" She had a point!) We are encouraged to seek wisdom, but we also must make sure we follow the will of God. When we ran this idea to them, I will never forget what Harold angrily said: "When will you stop chasing rainbows?" We were taken back a bit; he didn't usually show signs of disapproval so strongly. I know the price was more than what we were comfortable with, and I know it needed work, but we had vision! He told us that we needed to keep praying about our decision and that he and his wife would continue to pray for us as well. He also said he would pray that we would find something next to them in their hometown!

The rose-colored glasses were hindering some of the negative aspects of the house. For the money they were asking, it probably would take us a lifetime to bring back the original beauty and splendor of this place. The house needed a great deal of renovation to meet our standards of living. And the barn was collapsing. Our optimism of restoring something was a daunting task. We would rather fix it up than tear it down and start all over. I think we get that trait from our Heavenly Father. He repairs what's broken and restores. He doesn't throw us away. He transforms us.

I guess the only way to describe my desire for this house would be to compare it to someone who has an addiction problem with no self-control. The feeling is probably as strong as someone who lusts for a fix. I really did believe God put this dream into our hearts, but I wasn't trusting fully. I wasn't willing to lose this one. I wouldn't surrender to the will of God. My will was stubborn and relentless.

Right away, there were a few things that seemed "sketchy," but we quickly dismissed them. Everything was going as planned. We had to go through a nontraditional bank for the financing because it was such a unique property. The bank did finally approve us; they worked with a wide variety of farms and agriculture properties. We didn't expect to pay the appraiser two thousand dollars, though! Usual price was around six hundred bucks! They explained that the appraiser had to inspect the property and walk the entire acreage, and that it is often difficult for them to determine a true value because these properties are so sparse.

The good news is, we did sell our mini mansion! It happened to be to a guy we knew! He was on my honey's softball team (the one with the prison uniforms). We were so delighted to sell our masterpiece to someone we knew. We didn't put any conditions on the listing either. We were confident that the transaction would go smooth and uneventful.

Then we got a call from the lending institution. She apologized and told us the bank refused to loan us the money for our dream home. She told us the appraiser went into the basement and noticed a new concrete floor that was poured. After badgering the real estate agent for the seller, she finally admitted there was a prior oil spill. Oh, and the house had sewage pouring out onto the rear of the property. *What? This can't be happening! What are we going to do now? Our house is ready to close, and now we have no place to go!* I refused to give up. I didn't care if there was 150 gallons of oil under that house; I still wanted it! (I was lacking reason, and instead of being grateful that God could be sparing me grief, I stubbornly thought I could fix the contamination. Not a wise decision—it was stupidity!) No bank was going to loan us money for this property, and we certainly didn't have close to three hundred thousand dollars hanging around. Why did this stuff happen to us? Why were we being so risky? This was not just our lives anymore; we have three small children to think of. Was I being punished for my lack of gratitude for the mini mansion? Was I supposed to give up on our dreams? Was I sure those dreams were put in our hearts from God, or was this a mirage from Satan? Truth is, this house became an idol. And we bit the bait, hook, line, and sinker. Maybe we deserved what we got. How do you know the difference between faith and foolishness?

I know this sounds ridiculous, but being parents to three little ones gives us the excuse to enjoy Disney movies. If you've ever watched *Ferdinand* (the big black bull), then maybe you remember the part where he is frolicking around the hilly meadow with miniature flowers and sits by the large colossal tree in the pasture. The song titled "Home" by Nick Jonas is being played. Have you ever listened to the lyrics? "Home, no more running... I'm good knowing that I belong." To describe the place I was in when I saw that movie, it broke me down to tears. And of course, I was doing everything in my power to be discreet, not making any sudden movements, trying to flick the tears from my eyes, and holding my breath as drips came down the bridge of my nose. I didn't want the kids to see me respond to a cartoon so seriously, but my heart ached for that feeling. To find home, a place we belonged. I was beginning to wonder if the home that I yearned for was my heavenly home and that finding that "place" on earth was never supposed to happen.

abandoned

Jesus replied, "Have I been with you all this time, Phillip, and yet
you still don't know who I am? Anyone who has seen me has seen
the Father! So why are you asking me to show him to you?"

—John 14:9 NLT

I love Jesus, and I'm intimate with the Holy Spirit, but if I were honest, my relationship with the Father is elusive. I can't entirely wrap
my mind around the fact that all Three are One, but I do believe in
the Trinity. I wish I could say I know my Heavenly Father well and
completely trust Him, but if I were truthful, I still struggle after all
these years. I do desire to understand the Father fully, and sometimes
I may get a glimpse, but mostly I'm reserved and leery.

From the perspective of a naive young girl, I just believed what
my mother told me. She always used to tell us she was both our
mother *and* our father. And without question, I just assumed she was
telling me the truth. One day as I was sitting outside on the lawn
playing with my doll in front of our apartment building on Plane
Street in Worcester, I was approached by a stranger. He asked me
where my mom was. I told him she was upstairs. He tried to explain
to me that he was my father. I confidently said, "No, you're not. My
father is upstairs!" That was the first time I remember meeting my
biological father. As comical as it seems, I find it quite sad as I am
much older now.

My "father" never married my mother. I wouldn't say she was
exactly the marrying kind back then. The only time I really formed
much of an opinion about the man was by the way my mom would

speak about him. There wasn't much good that she had to say other than he was nice-looking then, had long hair, and could play the guitar. He was married to a nice, soft-spoken woman, and together (if I'm not mistaken) they had a total of eight children. My mom used to get so frustrated because he didn't help us out financially. She never received child support. Understandably, she used to get so angry that he would have all these additional children and have no consequence to abandoning me and my sister. Being a mom now helps me truly appreciate the magnitude of responsibility she had for three children alone. I have a challenging time myself, and that's with an amazing partner and responsible provider!

You don't miss something you've never had, right? I'm not so sure about that. The absence of knowing a "daddy" has made me unbalanced. I know how to be strong, but I don't know how to be vulnerable. I know how to survive, but maybe I don't know how to trust. Most of the women in my life had to become ruthless and resourceful. Yes, I've seen brides on their wedding day being escorted down the aisle by a father figure, and it's beautiful to have that relationship with an honorable man. But even on those occasions, I struggle with wholesome thoughts. I can't quite grasp what it might feel like because I have no memory of my own to go by. It trickles down into my marriage too. I have inadvertently treated the man of my life like he's the enemy, taking out my insecurities on him.

It gets worse. The things my mom shared with me when I was young about her father ruined my impression of fatherhood completely. Her story is not mine to tell; however, it affected me negatively and left a lot of fear and torment within my thinking about men. I was devastated. The man she described could not be the same person we would look forward to visiting. The man I knew was great with kids, sober, hardworking, funny, and musically talented. I had mixed emotions about my grandfather. I hated who he was, but I loved who he had become.

I probably would have lost all hope on fatherhood until I got to witness my husband be all a father should be. He blesses, protects, stands ground, doesn't threaten to run, provides, loves unconditionally, teaches, prays, encourages, spends time with our boys, sacrifices, has a generous spirit, and believes in them. Well, perhaps I do know the Father after all. Maybe my husband's example as a dad is similar to what my Heavenly Father must be like.

Pit Stop

*Jesus replied, "You don't understand now what
I am doing, but someday you will."*

—John 13:7 NLT

When your dreams slip through your fingers, it's hard to look at the bright side of things. I should have been grateful we even had a place to land. My honey had been working on an investment property for months in hopes to secure ourselves financially for our future. Being self-employed all these years and living way above our means didn't leave anything in the piggy bank for our retirement years. We wanted to try being landlords again. This was an ideal property! It was a five-family. The owner lived out of state and was sick of putting money into the building, so he sold it to us way below value. It required an extreme makeover. But my honey and his crew picked up their tools and painstakingly worked to turn this place into a money-making machine! Again the place was done right. Herb knew if we wanted to own this building and have tenants, we didn't want our tenants to have anything to complain about. We happened to have one apartment left that was open. We never knew God would make us neighbors with our tenants! My honey and the crew busted it double-time to get us in before the sale closed on our mini mansion.

I was angry and disappointed with God. I was humiliated. Here we are, living in an apartment building when all I could think of was the farmhouse that we should be unpacking in. It was a messy time for us. My dwarf apple tree was in a bucket, and our dog was in a cage outside. That was challenging because we had a strict policy of no animals, and there we were, bringing our dog! I didn't want to have to get rid of her; what would we tell the kids? We gave our chickens away to Herb's brother Sean. Everyone felt the effects of gambling our mini mansion away. I think I would have just settled there for the rest of our lives if I knew this was going to be the outcome! My faith was being tested. I hated living in an apartment. I had to use our coin-operated washing machine and dryer downstairs in the main utility room (poor me, we got the quarters back). We also shared the common backyard with the residents. It forced me to become social. Our tenants were decent people. I hated them seeing me so miserable. I was depressed and often wore my bathrobe. I couldn't pull myself out of the pit. I turned for the worst.

There were a couple of younger boys who lived in the apartment beside us who loved to play with ours. My mother-in-law stayed a few nights a week at our place and a few nights at her sister's to give us the much-needed space and time to process. Don't get me wrong; the place was clean, completely new, and provided everything that we needed. I felt guilty for being so immature and ungrateful, but it was never going to be our home. We knew that. We only unpacked what we needed. I felt consumed by fear and requested help from Pastor Ron's wife, Sherry. I was taken back when she told me, "I'm sorry, I can't help you." For years she has been my go-to gal. She helped me through times of difficulty. She recommended I see the church therapist. I knew my whole life I probably could have benefitted by getting counsel, but pride was a factor, along with trust issues. I didn't care at this point. I was so broken I wouldn't refuse any help. I was full of despair.

The day I walked into my first session was interesting. I came prepared with my pen and notebook. I met a seventy-something four-foot powerhouse for God named Shirley. She was shorter than I was! She had a walker, smelled like mothballs, and had a sweet tone in her voice. My first impression of her years ago at a women's weekend away was critical. I was less than impressed with her ability to recite the Bible word for word. She could memorize pages of scripture. I gave myself permission to be vulnerable and to trust her. I felt God's peace during our time together. I was grateful for her wisdom, her listening ear, and her suggestions.

She gave me an assignment that I wrote in my notebook. The next time we met up, I remember picking up from our last monthly session. She asked me if I did my homework. I was puzzled and confused. I was eager to please her and sought her approval. I was always a good student, and I wanted to prove that I was ready to submit. I was ready to roll up my sleeves and willing to do what needed to be done to end the torment I was suffering. She said to me, "Kristi, it's okay. It must not have been important to you, or you would have remembered it." It wasn't okay! I was adamant that she must be mistaken. She didn't give me any assignment! She graciously said, "Take a peek at your notes." And so I flipped through the pages and noticed that, in my own handwriting, there was, in fact, a lesson for me to complete.

I cried. I felt like a failure. I wanted to get this process going. I didn't want to waste her time or my own. I think she realized then that I was suffering from PTSD. That was when we started to go over more of my physical and medical problems. She suggested I make an appointment with my doctor right away.

I went on to describe to her in full detail the range of events that took place in my life that eventually brought me to her. She spoke life into me and told me that God has a calling on my and my husband's life. Even though she didn't know me that well, she continued to say that our family was a beautiful example. That marked the beginning of a special relationship.

I visited my mom and asked her if she would help me get through some details of my past. I pleaded with her that I couldn't remember most of my childhood and that I blacked out a lot. There was hesitation at first, but she reassured me that even if it caused her to suffer, she would do it for me because she loved me. We have gone over the past together so many times. We wanted to move on. We wanted new memories, something different to reminisce about. But I felt like I needed to go over things with her one last time. I wanted to get to the root of my issues so that I could finally be healed and set free.

My mom began talking about how it didn't surprise her how many times I moved because when I was little, we moved a lot too.

She said we lived in many towns: Spencer, Charlton, Oxford, and North Brookfield. I remembered the first three towns, but not North Brookfield. I asked her about how old I was and where in North Brookfield. She said she moved in with a friend named Rhonda, but it was only for a short time. I was probably around five years old, give or take. The house should have been condemned then! She said the place used to give her the creeps. She told me it was a large multifamily! When she revealed the street name, it sent shivers up my spine, and my whole body had goose bumps!

I said, "Mom, are you talking about the five-family?"

She said, "Yes."

I said, "You do know that is the very place we are living in right now!"

I told her we bought the place months ago and renovated it to rent. We both were at a loss for words! It all started to make sense to me now.

I explained the details word for word to Shirley. She noticed when I spoke about the apartment that I had intense fear. She stopped me and said we needed to pray right then. She asked me if I ever discussed selling the five-family with my honey. I told her that we had discussed it, but it would be a shame to let it go because we were profiting over $3,000 a month; and when we get into our older years, that could be a means of income and eventually be something we could pass on to our children.

She strongly told me she felt we were supposed to sell it. I called my honey on the way home and shared with him what was said. As much as it would torture us to sell it, my honey aired on the side of being obedient to Christ. He never wanted to meet Jesus in heaven and be told that he was in rebellion. So the very next day, we had a verbal agreement with a good friend who showed interest in the house before we renovated it. He already had multiple properties for rent. He asked my honey, "Are you sure? Why would you sell this place? It's making such good income." It was painful, but we sold it within a month. There went our investment for our future. Resentment and regret were brewing.

Lord Have Mercy!

Are any of you sick? You should call for the elders of the church to come and pray over you, anointing you with oil in the name of the Lord.

—James 5:14 NLT

My friend Emma was diagnosed with breast cancer back in July of 2015, so when my health began to deteriorate, I knew she would be someone I could go to. She would stay in contact with me, and we would compare levels from our blood-work results. I don't feel like I was calloused when she told me the horrible news; I just had this hopeful feeling she was going to pull through.

She is an incredibly strong, resourceful woman. She deserved the senior superlative of best personality with my honey in high school. She was a smart, determined person, so I had no doubt she was going to win this war. She was the kind of person you could vent to. She gave helpful advice and was a great pep talker if you were in much need of encouragement. I loved her blatant honesty and her sarcastic sense of humor. Even though she was in the middle of difficulty, she still found time to reach out to others. She was often the facilitator of our girls' nights outs with Tina and Marsha. We would exchange parental tips, financial resources, and nutrition ideas. I really don't know how she was able to work full-time, commute over an hour one way, be a mom to two daughters, a wife, and the many other hats she wears. She was the energizer bunny! One quirky pet peeve I have of her was that she had a difficult time making decisions. She would drive a hasty person batty! When she was trying to decide a color selection to paint in her living room, she was methodical and patient. She had a variety of different paint swatches marking the interior walls. Knowing we were going to dinner together at a restaurant, you better not go hungry. You never knew how long it was gonna take before she ordered her meal! I think it took her three days to finally name her second daughter! One of Emma's favorite desserts was from yours truly, my pumpkin cheesecake!

Your body slowly whispers to you when it's in need of something; at least mine did for a while. I kept ignoring symptoms. I didn't have time to be sick! It was inconvenient. I felt guilty if I couldn't keep up. It messed with me physically, mentally, emotionally, and spiritually. I valued myself on my abilities. I took pride in being busy and having a full life. My body refused to be ignored; it was screaming at me! The years of abuse and neglect revealed itself through a list of symptoms. For privacy purposes, I will only list some. You have to remember, I'm just forty-two years old. I don't smoke cigarettes, I rarely have a glass of wine (maybe just a handful of times a year), and I don't do drugs. I am only on one prescription for thyroid issues I inherited, but other than that, I think I take pretty good care of myself for the most part. I know I don't get enough exercise, that's for sure. I'm not as disciplined as I wish I am. Exercise is on the bottom of my list of priorities. I don't drink water as much as I probably should, and even though I'm a believer, I still worry! I am stressed out a lot! Oh yeah, and I don't go to bed usually before 11:00 p.m.

So here was the list of problems I suffered from: low/no energy, fatigue, exhaustion, eye twitching for months, gut issues, acne, heart palpitations, anxiety attacks, nervous energy, hot/cold spells (very sensitive to cold), sound sensitivity (ears would ring for months), hypothyroidism, body tremors, irritability (low patience levels), head pressure and headaches, dizziness, psoriasis behind my left ear on my scalp for over a year, low vitamin D levels, low iron, anemia, poor memory, difficulty concentrating (this was one of the worst), eye pressure and sun sensitivity, low white blood cells for over a year and a half, colitis, low blood pressure, recent dairy allergy, and many other things I will spare you the details on, but you get the picture. I just didn't feel good for a really long time!

I played the doctor shuffle for a while. First, I went to my primary doctor. He had been concerned because when he did an EKG, he noticed my heart was having unusual patterns. He sent me for a stress test, but that came back fine. Then he ran blood work, lots of it. There was the beginning of the doctor merry-go-round! I was referred to a gastroenterologist. He ran tests and suggested I swallow a PillCam and have a colonoscopy. Oh goody (I never would have agreed to this procedure, but I was so desperate for answers). That's when it was confirmed I had colitis and a milk allergy. I was thankful the two biopsies came back fine. He also gave me antibiotics in case I had giardia. After that suggestion, I still suffered, so I was sent over to a hematologist. I was frustrated because I had to see my doctor at the "Cancer Center." When I went to check in, I was scared. Why was I being sent here? Was there something the doctors weren't telling me? Should I be worried? I saw a bald woman (younger than I was) sitting in the waiting room. I prayed for her that God would heal her and spare her life while I wondered what was going on. I hated the name of that building! Who would want to go there? Why couldn't they name it the Healing Center? Or the Hope for Health Center? What's wrong with people?

The receptionist must have known I was disturbed. She told me that my doctor works on many different patients with blood issues; not everyone was a cancer patient. So after many months of monitoring my blood work and adjusting iron supplements, my number stayed significantly low. It was confusing to go to an educated professional for help, and they seemed more baffled than I was. The doctor asked me if my white blood cells were always low. How would I know? So with some research, I located my blood results after Little Herbie was born, and the range was normal. I was glad I could share that information with him at my next visit. I didn't want him to just dismiss me as "normally low" if, in fact, I had an issue. Then I was sent to infectious disease specialist. As much as I respect doctors, this was a joke! I felt like I was being treated as an imbecile! She didn't listen to me; apparently everyone fits into the same category. Basically, since I didn't visit Africa, I was fine. She dismissed everything I had to say. *Next!*

Then I got bounced to a rheumatology doctor. Do you know how long it takes to finally get an appointment to see these doctors?

Sometimes it takes months. So while I was being passed around like a hot potato, my symptoms were getting worse, and I was growing more agitated. Not to mention there were times I asked my honey to schedule my appointments around his workday so he could be there for me while I had Joey. As we were strolling Joey through the doors to the rheumatology doctor's office, we waited in line for a bit. Then when it was my turn to check in, the receptionist said, "Oh, I'm sorry, your appointment has been cancelled. Did you not get the message?" I was furious! I was unwell; I needed someone to help me! My face must have said a thousand words because the woman behind the receptionist asked to see me privately. She told me that the doctor I was supposed to see no longer works there and that she would help me see the person who replaced her that day, but it might just take a while. I had been waiting for the doctor to explain my blood results for a couple months now. Self-diagnosing from the Google search engine is not wise! It seemed likely something autoimmune was going on. I wanted answers so I could find a cure, a remedy.

I appreciated her compassion, and when I finally spoke to the doctor, she said that even though I tested positive for rheumatoid factor and had a speckled ANA, I did not have rheumatoid arthritis (I read somewhere if you have a speckled ANA result, it could be lupus). I asked her about lupus; she said she didn't believe that I had that either but that she would follow up with further testing. Then it was suggested that I have a CT scan. After that test, the doctor saw something near the right side of my brain, so he ordered another one. That evening, I noticed a rash developing around my neck after the procedure. I told my doctor, and he mentioned that most likely I had an adverse reaction to the contrast dye.

Months later, my primary physician requested another CT scan. I remember filling out preliminary paperwork while I was in the waiting room. The doctor who was about to perform my scan kneeled next to me and told me he wasn't going to do the procedure. He said he couldn't believe my doctor recommended the procedure to be done without Benadryl and other safety precautions. He told me he had witnessed a few patients die on the table because they were allergic to the dye. I was so confused and thankful I had my mind about me that day to write in on my paperwork that I did have a reaction the last time. No doubt again, God was watching over me. I never went back for the scan. Then I got another suggestion to go to the neurologist (for the eye twitching and headaches). I refused by this point. I was so sick and tired of doctors passing me around. I needed a break. It was probably a year and a half of running around chasing my tail.

Finally, I asked the Lord, "What is wrong with me? Why is my body so sick?" And here the answer came: *Kristi, you need to forgive.* He showed me the verse in the Bible that says if anyone is sick, then go to the elders of the church and have them pray over you and anoint your head with oil. I couldn't believe it could be that simple! Well, I've tried every concoction and remedy I could find, some a little crazier than others: lemon water, turmeric, protein and green shakes, chia seeds, enemas, aloe vera juice, liver, candida and parasite cleanses, zapper electrotherapy, probiotics, prebiotics, enzymes, cod-liver oil, flax seed oil, coconut oil—the list goes on and on, I even took myself off oral contraception (for heavy periods) and ingested food-grade diatomaceous earth! While some things did seem to help, this biblical remedy is something I haven't tried yet!

I hoped Pastor Ron would allow me this opportunity. I had never seen him or the deacons doing anything like this before. Only a few times have we even held a healing service. This was very specific. I was thankful when he agreed. So after church service, Pastor Ron, Pastor Kole, and a few of the deacons and their wives prayed over us and asked for God to bring healing to my body and to our family. My honey was also suffering for months with an enlarged spleen and a couple other issues. Pastor Ron opened the bottle of oil from the kitchen. He anointed my head, my honey's, and our boys'. I felt God's peace and reassurance that everything was going to be okay.

I couldn't believe I was referred back to the first doctor I saw, the gastroenterologist. He suggested I take another test that he hadn't given me yet: a breath test. He said it wasn't a common diagnosis, but if I tested positive, it was an easy fix with an antibiotic that usually helps clear it up. Lo and behold, I tested positive for SIBO (small-intestine bacterial overgrowth). You're kidding me! I took the prescribed medications for three weeks and noticed a great deal of issues began to disappear!

It wasn't overnight, but healing did happen. When I went to the hematology appointment, the doctor reviewed the results of my recent blood work and, with a smile, asked me what I did differently. Unashamed, I told him, "God healed me." He looked at me and said, "No, really, what have you been doing differently?" I smiled and repeated the words to him, "God healed me!" I didn't want to be arrogant, but I could tell his beliefs were different from mine; and maybe because he was a doctor, he seemed to desire definitive scientific answers, not supernatural testimony. I was hoping he would ask me to elaborate; I had already told him of God's hand in my life with infertility. He said he didn't feel the need to see me in three months. He pushed out the next appointment for a follow-up in twelve.

Then a purging began to take place.

Frugal Forgiver

Therefore, if you are offering your gift at the altar and there remember that your brother or sister has something against you, leave your gift there in front of the altar. First go and be reconciled to them; then come and offer your gift.

—Matthew 5:23–24 NLT

I don't believe every case of illness is caused by bitter unforgiveness, but I do believe it can stem from it. Sometimes I can presume I am blameless (innocent of wrongdoing) in the eyes of God. If God knows my every thought, every motive, and every action, I know I need to just be honest with Him and confess to Him the things He brings to the surface. Please don't mistake blameless with sinless! As much as I know the Word says we are forgiven as far as the east is from the west, I still desire to obey God, but my flesh is very weak! The apostle Paul describes me perfectly in Romans 7:15–20 NLT:

> I don't really understand myself, for I want to do is right, but I don't do it. Instead, I do what I hate. But if I know what I am doing is wrong, this shows that I agree that the law is good. So, I am not the one doing wrong; it is sin living in me that does it. And I know that nothing good lives in me, that is, in my sinful nature. I want to do what is right, but I can't. I want to do what is good, but I don't. I don't want to do what is wrong, but I do it anyway. But if I do what I

don't want to do, I am not really the one doing
wrong; it is sin living in me that does it.

Even though there's truth in those verses, it's still extremely difficult to admit it.

God says when we fail to forgive others, our Father in heaven will not forgive us. But what if we *think* we have? I have had the honor of worshiping Jesus on and off now for over a decade with our worship team at our church. I know I originally made fun of the corny music, but God has ironically changed my heart! Only God can give us courage and ability to use the gifts He equips us with. I used to be so fearful singing in front of crowds. Remember when I felt I needed to supplement alcohol with singing in my early years? Now, as long as I'm focused on Him and my heart is right, I have the ability to sing with our team in a room full of over a hundred people! I'm telling you, it's miraculous. It was always a hope that I could share my voice with others in a confident way, not jittery and self-conscious. When I was young, I can remember wanting to sing at a talent show and my music teacher telling me I had a nice voice. I reluctantly chose the song "Mama He's Crazy" by the Judds. Well, unfortunately, I was way too young to reach those low notes; and when I sang, I was so afraid and timid I couldn't continue. I just stood there in front of the other kids during practice and cried. I was so humiliated.

There's no better connection for me than when I am plugged into the Holy Spirit. He meets me there every time without fail. I have been so sick at times I thought I would faint. I would look for an escape route just in case I felt the need to vomit. I didn't want to step down just because I was pregnant, had morning sickness, or was under the weather. I loved being a part of the whole congregation. I love when I witness God move others to cry, raise their hands to the heavens, or sing joyously out loud along with us. It's a beautiful experience and privilege.

I was convicted when I read the verses from Matthew 5:23–24. I really knew in my heart God was showing me that I needed to step down from the worship team and make an effort to reconcile with a relative I have been harboring hidden resentment with. With much prayer, I felt this particular person probably wouldn't meet with me face-to-face, even if I had good intentions. I struggled with confronting her because I didn't want to be shut down. I vented a lot and fell into the sin of gossip. I wanted others to hear my side of the story; I wanted to be heard. I wasn't able to sit idly and feel the blow of the verbal punches. I wanted to be defended. I wasn't trusting God. The consequences had caused great grief and disappointment among many of us.

Notice the scripture doesn't say leave your gift at the altar if *you* have something against someone. It says leave your gift at the altar if you know someone else has something against *you*! That was clear because I heard from others; a lot was being said. I used to be so close to this relative. I loved her and missed her companionship. We had a lot of special memories. Remember when Madam Jean instilled fear in my honey about motorcycles? We gained courage and refused to allow that to have power over us. When we lived at the Cape many years ago, we bought a Harley-Davidson motorcycle and used to ride a lot with this person and her husband. I have so many awesome memories! Riding down to Daytona during bike week and coasting through the Florida Keys, even driving through the Everglades. Those times were so special to us, but none of that mattered anymore. I was basically written off.

Any time someone hurt her, she wouldn't engage; she just ignored that person like they never existed. It was painful. So I wrote a seventeen-page letter with deep love and humility. I paid for postage and dropped the thick envelope into the slot at the post office. I prayed she would receive it, open it, and that it would repair any hurt that I had caused and perhaps mend our strained relationship. I can't force someone to trust. I can't force someone to love. And I certainly can't force someone to forgive! At the next family holiday, she didn't utter a word to me. I knew I did my part and what was expected of me by God, and even though we didn't communicate, I know if God allows that to happen someday, it will be up to Him. I'm open to restoration if it is His will. I envision us having a cup of tea together just like we used to.

Just as much as I've needed to forgive others, I know I've needed to receive it too! It goes to show you how evil even a child's intentions can be. I remember as far back as being elementary-school-aged listening in on adult conversations that I probably had no business hearing. When I heard my mom talking about a cousin of mine (whom I loved and looked up to) not being my uncle's daughter biologically, I couldn't wait to let the cat out of the bag. I had a bit of jealousy for her because she was "daddy's angel," and she never had a want for anything. When we were on a playground across my aunt's house in Spencer, that's when I repeated what I heard. At first, as those words came out of my mouth, I was so satisfied at telling her the big secret. But it was her response that I could never forgive myself for. She was crushed and very upset and went running to her mom to ask if what I said was true. That's not the way a child should hear such information. I felt the worst. The strange thing was, I didn't need to be punished for my actions—I already felt bad enough for not controlling my tongue.

As time passes on, you sometimes forget that kind of stuff. Well, when I was pregnant with Benjamin, I was reminded by the Holy Spirit. I couldn't believe He was telling me to say sorry. This was decades later! As uncomfortable as it was for me to bring it up, I did. I asked her to forgive me for being so cruel as a child, that what I did was inexcusable. I told her how sorry I was. We cried and hugged. She seemed to brush it off. How did I deserve such grace? I didn't! So what if someone reinjures you? How many times are we supposed to forgive? Matthew 18:21–22 says, "Then Peter came to him and asked, 'Lord, how often should I forgive someone who sins against me? Seven times?' 'No, not seven times,' Jesus replied, 'but seventy times seven!'" I'll tell you, that ain't easy! I'm all about justice and consequences, although I do appreciate grace and mercy when I'm in the wrong! And no, I don't think we're supposed to be someone's doormat. If you're being abused, I wouldn't recommend staying in that environment and accepting that behavior; that's not the evidence of forgiveness. Bottom line is, as good as it is to be frugal, it's not good to be a frugal forgiver! With the help of God, I'm working on becoming a *frequent* forgiver!

Healed Scars

If I must boast, I will boast of the things that show my weakness.

—2 Corinthians 11:30 NIV

On the bottom of my right foot, there is still evidence of a small lump from something that took place over thirty years ago. I was spending time with my family in Vermont, and I used to carry my cousin Little Marky on my hip when he was just a toddler. I was walking outside and felt a cold sensation shoot up from the bottom of my foot. I had a decision to make in a split second: Do I drop the child to save myself, or do I cling onto the child and endure the long rusty nail that was hidden under a piece of wood?

I made the right decision, and even though I suffered, my younger cousin was protected. I went into the house and had to soak my foot in a bucket. It was a small sacrifice out of love for a child. I took that nail for him! Jesus sacrificed His entire life knowingly and willingly. He wanted to spare us from certain eternal death. He painfully accepted three long excruciating nails that pierced Him and attached His horrifically beaten body to a cross, which eventually led to a miserable death. His death symbolizes the love He has for us. He took those nails for you and me!

"But He was pierced for our rebellion, crushed for our sins. He was beaten so we could be whole. He was whipped so we could be healed" (Isaiah 53:5 NLT). Why? So we could be healed! Incomprehensible love! We can never say we don't know anyone who would give up their life for us. Even though He had the power to save Himself, He didn't! He loves us that much!

Most of us have scars. Some of us show them off and call for a bragging session, and some of us wish they could be erased. I had three Cesarean sections to prove the birth of our children. I also have a tiny oval that displays darker pigmentation on my shin from Ray when I worked at the bank. He thought it would be funny to spray me with the compressed air that's made to dust electronic equipment!

The inch-long vertical line above my lip reminds me of when my brother, Nathan, dropped our cat Pearl out of our apple tree. With extended claws, she landed on my face! My honey has a hook-shaped scar on his scalp. When he was a young boy, he was cornered by a German shepherd, and it literally ripped off his ear! He had 144 stitches! Our son Benjamin was the first child to get stitches, not a surprise! He was playing at an outdoor playground, lost his footing, and fell face-first. Poor Mimi, she called us while we were on date night. We met her at a parking lot and brought him to the hospital. He wasn't in tears like I expected. His right eye was bloody, and he ended up with four stitches. He kept asking me if I would send the picture to his teacher.

Emma, my friend who won the battle to breast cancer, asked me if I would like to see her new tattoos. At first, I thought it was odd because she's not the body-ink type. Then it came to me: she was showing me the replacement of what was lost through the reconstructive surgeries. I was honored she felt that comfortable and trusting to reveal herself to me. Her vulnerability showed strength and courage. It made me think, would I be able to share such intimate personal details with her? Most people hide their imperfections (including myself). Tactfully, she exposed her skin. There was no shame. I was impressed with the quality of work that had been done. It's one thing to hear when your friend is having multiple surgeries. It's another when you see the scars and evidence of patchwork around her torso. I had a newfound respect for her that day. I was given a visual map of explanation as she pointed to some of the skin that was removed from her belly and reworked in other areas. The fact that she was alive to tell me was such a victory and testament to God's goodness. He didn't allow her to be taken down!

Every scar has a story. Some scars are emotional, which means they are invisible. Just because they can't be seen doesn't mean they're not there. Sometimes when we are reinjured, it can feel like a scab was ripped off from an old wound. Unfortunately, that's usually when the healing process takes a lot longer.

My cell phone had alarms every time a new house went up for sale. On one of our date nights, it was only eleven minutes in when a contemporary split-level ranch came on the market in North Brookfield. We both decided to ride by. It was starting to get dark. We thought we would schedule with our realtor an appointment the following day to walk around. I really think she thought we were crazy! It was nicely decorated and smelled like Yankee candles. There were nine acres of land in a heavily wooded lot on a rural quiet road. It was less than twelve years old and had a lot of room, 2,800 square feet. We were so tired of being bounced around, and my honey knew the importance of getting me out of the apartment (my sanity depended on it). I suggested to my honey that since there was such a great amount of space, we could bless his mom with her own portion of the home. We had been living together for about three years, and the lines were getting blurred on what her position was with our boys. I heard one of our sons mention he had three parents, and that just didn't fly well with me. I was missing the five of us and desired our own living space. There really wasn't much to choose from in the towns we were searching in, and the market was very competitive. You didn't have a lot of time to make up your mind; they were selling like hot cakes! We decided to try the mortgage company that our neighbor from the mini mansion worked for. She was a branch manager, and we needed all the favors we could find. Losing the loan from the "decoy" property in Warren didn't help our credit report. She preapproved us.

My honey didn't communicate with me first and bypassed our realtor (he didn't mean any disrespect; we love her dearly). He verbally offered the woman who was selling her home 23K less than the asking price. The owner was also her own realtor. He wasn't playing games. He cut through the small talk and shared with her our story. I think it touched her heart. She and her husband had two sons grow up in the house. She told us she would give us an answer by 5:00 p.m. She had another person scheduled to take a look that day. We were pleased to find out she accepted our offer. She told us that someone else put in the full offer but that she wanted to see us move in with our family. I felt beyond blessed that she would take our offer over the other person's and lose the extra profit. I chalked that up to God's grace. Our neighbor pulled through and executed a closing within thirty days! We were so anxious to finally move into a home again with lots of room and privacy. Hope and gratitude filled my veins. I felt like I had life coming back to me. Knowing we had a house to move into gave me the ability to wait out the next few weeks.

Every time we moved boxes of our belongings, Sean (Herb's brother) had bets that we wouldn't last more than two years. We planted our dwarf apple tree and prayed it would survive yet another transplant. The boys were so easy to please. We renovated a couple rooms to accommodate Mimi with her new independent place. We still spent a great deal of time together and would invite her regularly for dinners.

I hated being in the shade, so my honey found a tree-removal company to cut down a lot of the tall trees away from the house. It gave us a huge open yard for the kids and their four-wheelers. We planted gardens, put up a greenhouse, and my honey had the largest deck off the side of the house constructed. He also mortared another brick firewall and installed a woodstove—again! I loved the open space. The kitchen and living room were completely open with vaulted ceilings. Even though we vowed we weren't going to repaint the walls, we couldn't help it. We wanted to personalize our home again. We took advantage of installing solar panels on the roof. We refused to ever move again! We were done. We were going to just accept the fact that we were probably not meant to be in a large farmhouse. This was it. We found contentment for a while. We learned from YouTube how to make our own maple syrup from the abundance of trees we had on the property. Sean knew how much I loved to collect décor that had anything to do with farm animals and handed me a cow dinner bell. He told me to hang it up when we find the farmhouse we've always searched for. I shoved it in the back of my closet with a smirk on my face.

One day Sean called my honey. He said he needed a ride to the hospital; something strange was happening. He thought he might be having a stroke. My honey was already en route and had the boys with him, so I met him in the parking lot at the hospital to grab the boys while Sean went in to get checked. After multiple tests, the MRI showed he did, in fact, have two strokes! One happened previously without him knowing. Sean was only thirty-nine at the time. It was a close call. Thankfully, God spared his life. We've noticed he seems to appreciate life more and lets go of the petty things that used to stress him out.

My honey attended an Iron Sharpens Iron event with some men from our church. He was so pumped up when he came home. He told me he knew what God was calling him to do. I said, "Uh-oh, what now?" He asked me, "You know how we've been waiting for God to supply a boys' ministry with the church?" For many years, there has been an anointed ministry for young girls, but for some odd reason, not boys. Every time someone new would visit our church, we would scope them out as a potential leader for this imaginary group we were hoping for. Our boys were coming to the age range of benefiting from such a ministry. Casually, I even volunteered my honey for the potential position to Bonnie. I thought if leadership in the church was recruiting, maybe someone might approach him with the opportunity. Years passed by.

My honey told me it was crystal clear to him that he was chosen to lead the group. I wasn't surprised at all. He's really amazing with our boys! He was so excited and inspired by the first season of events. The details were falling into his lap. He was appreciative by the support he was receiving from the men of our church offering to help volunteer as mentors and team leaders. Our mission is to reach boys from first through sixth grade with a biblical hands-on lesson. We want to teach boys that God made them to be strong and courageous. I'll give you a couple examples. The highlighted scripture was from Matthew 17:20 NLT: "Jesus told them, 'I tell you the truth, if you had faith even as small as a mustard seed, you could say to this mountain, "Move from here to there," and it would move. Nothing would be impossible.'" The dads and male mentors (the male mentors were there for boys who did not have a dad) took the boys for a hike up a mountain! Another time, the boys went to Ultimate Obstacles (which is kind of like a ninja-warrior training area). The scripture that they focused on was from James 1:12 NLT: "God blesses those who patiently endure through testing and temptation. Afterward they will receive the crown of life that God has promised to those who love him." Every boy was awarded a king's crown! Each month is something completely different and fun. It's an outlet that Herb can pour his heart and creativity into.

We've seen God work miracles in such a short time with this ministry. There's a child we had been praying for many months whom we hadn't met yet. My mom shared his story with me out of concern. Then God assigned me to pray for him. He was living with his grandmother and had a troubled life. I introduced myself to the grandmother one day when I went to visit my mom. I told her we would love for her grandson to come to the boys' ministry if he was interested. She was receptive and appreciative. Since then, every month for almost two years, we travel in their neck of the woods and bring him to each event. What an incredible kid! He is extremely bright, loves every make and model of cars, and has street smarts. This light-skinned, freckled, carrot top has soft brown eyes that resembles his grandmother's. His accent is a cross between Bostonian and Southern. He gets along fine with our boys and is very respectful. He has been introduced to Jesus and is making great strides. There's no doubt in my mind God has an amazing plan for his life.

Hidden Treasure!

The Kingdom of Heaven is like a treasure that a man discovered hidden in a field. In his excitement, he hid it again and sold everything he owned to get enough money to buy the field. Again, the Kingdom of Heaven is like a merchant on the lookout for choice pearls. When he discovered a pearl of great value, he sold everything he owned and bought it!

—Matthew 13:44–46 NLT

The sale of our five-family put us in a bind. We never would have been approved to buy this 2,800-square-foot home without that additional income. Our tens of thousands in renovations to make our house a home didn't help either. We decided we were going to get serious about our finances. We bought a whiteboard and erasable markers and listed all our debts so we could see the balances together. We listed all of our assets and liabilities. What a wake-up call! What a big mess again! We went to dozens of classes on money management and listened to hours of teachings, but we always felt like our optimistic plans of becoming debt-free were ungraspable.

Maybe we just had tough luck. But as hard as we worked, we couldn't get ahead. Many times we didn't want to burden our financial counselors Harold and Jane anymore. We felt like a lost cause to all the times they invested in us over the years. Time to be extreme. We were gonna make things happen once and for all! So we took advice from Dave Ramsey one last time. We put $1,000 away for our "emergency fund" *again*. We started to pay off all our little credit cards, and instead of locking them up, we cut them up. We made painful decisions to give up the car and truck payments. I loved nice, dependable vehicles! We paid to get rid of them. Now we were driving jalopies. It was embarrassing. I didn't like picking the kids up from school in my rusted minivan. I cringed every time I turned the key over. Against my conscience, I even stopped paying AAA to save a few bucks. People looked at us funny! Even Christians! We tried to convince others of our debt-free goal, but I know people thought we were crazy. "Live like no one else so you can live like no one else"—I used to repeat Dave Ramsey's motto in a condescending manner to my honey when we would climb in our vehicle.

Steadily we were making progress. It pushed us to get even more aggressive with our approach. We called the shed rental company and told them they could pick up our leased sheds. That was another few hundred dollars a month saved. Why did we have a five thousand dollar shed for a few chickens? It just didn't make sense! For what? A couple dozen eggs?

If I were honest, I contemplated ixnaying on the tithing. I looked in the Bible for any excuse I could find where it was acceptable to use those funds for downing debt. I couldn't find permission anywhere! We had seen miracle after miracle over the years from being faithful (not perfect) tithers and opted to continue to trust God. After the decade of years owing Herb's brother Sean, we finally paid him in full! Once we received a check in the mail from a class-action lawsuit for $35,000, we handed it right over to Sean! It felt so good to look him in the eye and know we no longer were his slave! There was a time he even borrowed money from us. It felt so good to be the one lending for a change!

I'm sure some people may have said, if your finances are always causing you this much unsurety, why don't you hang it up and get a "real" job? Short answer is, we love what we do! It's not stress-free, but it gives us freedom that money can't buy. My honey has the ability to drive our boys to school most mornings (thankfully, Mimi alternates with us). He can attend their school concerts and shift his schedule around doctor's appointments. He can volunteer to coach their games and spend more time with them during the summer months. My honey has the leeway to plan vacations for as many days as we wish; there is no boss to tell him no (other than you-know-who!).

What if God has us right where He wants us? Give us this day our daily bread; we've never gone without. He faithfully gives us what we need every single day! Maybe we can accept that we will always be God-dependent, not independent of God or depending on an employer. Self-sufficiency is a farce! God supplies even the self-sufficient. It's a lot more difficult and requires residual faith to depend on His provision. Now, I'm not saying we can't be better stewards with what God has given us; there's always room for improvement. But is it possible to find contentment while you're still trying to achieve a status of financial security? We live off loans and pray every time we finish the rehabilitation of a house that it will sell and that we will make a profit. Sometimes we win, and sometimes we lose. We are paid a few times a year. Try budgeting that! We rack up most of the credit accounts and pay them off when it sells.

My honey was looking for another property. We were entertaining the thought of moving "one last time" (as long as it was going to give us the ability to live below our means). There was a house he mentioned to me that was on the market for under a hundred thousand dollars. Immediately I dismissed the idea. It was ugly, and there were tons of junk in the yard.

About a month later, I was scrolling through properties, and I brought up the same one he mentioned to me a month prior. He used to get so frustrated with me when I claimed the glory for a good idea that was originally his. The price was right, and there was "potential." He told me he'd been there once before and that there was five acres of land with a barn and outbuildings. That heightened my interest. "Why didn't you tell me that earlier?" I said. He said, "Kristi, I know the guy who lives there. I gave him a shed a couple years ago." No kidding!

The house was in the process of a foreclosure, and the bank had it listed. My honey took a ride and told me the guy welcomed him in to take a look around. He told him when cars came up to the driveway, he scared them away. He ran out with his phone and snapped pictures of the people who might be interested in the property. You see, he was squatting for years, living for free on someone else's tab. He was cordial with my honey. My honey asked him about some details of the property and questioned if we bought it, would he be willing to leave the premises in peace? He told him that we were looking for a home for our family, and we couldn't risk buying it if the man had no intentions of going any time soon. The man agreed. Seriously! (I know that's God's favor again!) So we took his word for it and (knowing there was risk) put in an offer. There was an offer before ours that someone retracted on. The deal was, you had to get rid of the tenant. Ouch! With laws out there, that could be a pretty penny of legal fees and a waste of time. We offered $4,900 less than the asking price, and our offer was accepted.

We weren't 100 percent sure if we were going to make it our home or flip it. We were keeping our options open, but it was a possibility. After we closed, the house of our dreams came on the market in North Brookfield! We took the kids for a ride and called our realtor to take a peek. There I went feening again! It was a historical colonial built in 1780! It had all the same desires as our "decoy" house, just less land and a smaller barn. There was one and a half acres, wide pine floors, three fireplaces, and a good-sized rear deck that had open sunlight from dawn to dusk. I loved the exposed beams in the kitchen! I was lured by the stone walls, a barn with a hayloft, a huge old tree, fruit trees, perennials, and I practically tripped over the vine of a watermelon! Here was the one we'd been waiting for! This had to be it! We were automatically thinking, *No big deal. We will just flip the other house and sell it. This is the one we will make our home!*

We were too late; an offer was already accepted. You think I'd know better by now not to get my hopes so high. I was quite confused, again. Why did I allow my emotions to be so easily manipulated? Maybe that was just a temptation, Lord knows we couldn't handle that again!

It took a little longer than we wanted it to, but eventually the man did keep his word and removed all his belongings and left the premises. He took his two horses, pet pig and all the piles of scrap metal. The bank gave him a financial incentive to go. We were very relieved and chalked that up to another favorable God moment.

The renovation started that fall, and the team worked through the winter months in harsh weather. My honey tried to renovate the house without dumping every penny into it. But when he opened the walls, there was no foundation on the addition. The floors were rotted. He tried to convince me to accept the house without the addition. As much as I tried, I couldn't envision our family in a "tiny" home. I didn't mind a small home, but we needed space. The ceilings we weren't going to replace had to be torn down; the windows we were going to save were pulled. We just couldn't convince ourselves to chince out on this house. We always renovated with integrity and made sure the job was complete to the same standards that we would expect in a home. If this was going to be our home, we couldn't possibly renovate it with our expectations of being debt-free. Something had to give.

Remember that historical colonial? The offer that they accepted fell through; we were next in line. They asked us if we still wanted to buy the property, so we took a ride by after church on Sunday, and I instigated. I dared my honey to go talk to the old buck in the barn. He said, "I'm not afraid!" I tried to bribe the kids to keep it down in the car as Herb spoke with the owner of the house. After the conversation, the old buck told my honey he liked him, and even though he was accepting offers for another few days, he called up his real estate agent right there and then and told them that he wanted to sell us the house! Cut it out! We didn't even have financing! He said he would hold the property for us for a few months till we sold our house that we were currently living in.

Unbelievable! How gracious! The old buck and his wife envisioned fixing the place up for years, but the project was over his head, and his wife had passed on since. My honey told him this was what we do for a living and that we would love to invite him when the renovation was complete so he could see it.

We went back and forth dozens of times. Was this house the one for us? Or was it the one we were currently working on? I know it may not sound like much of a problem, but it was tough making that decision. We asked the boys what their preference was and which house they could envision themselves in for the remainder of their childhood. We negotiated and promised them they wouldn't have to share rooms no matter which house we went to.

I admit, I did try to sway their decision. I bribed them to pick the house I wanted. But then I felt guilty because their wants were just as valid as mine. What if God was blessing us with either option? What if there wasn't a wrong decision? Now we had two farmhouses to choose from. Both were comparable. Both had a barn, land, a beautiful home—it was a matter of which one was better suitable for our future. I was so terrified to make the wrong decision; you remember what happened before! Whichever house we chose as a family, I wanted to finally be content! I wanted to feel like we were home! We even asked Mimi for her opinion; she wanted no part in the decision-making process. She was wise in staying neutral. I really clung to Little Herbie's opinion. He seemed to have the gift of discernment at an early age. He was so confident. When I asked him which one he thought belonged to us, without hesitation, he revealed it was the farmhouse we were already renovating with the five acres of land.

Tentatively, we leaned onto keeping the property with the five acres. Patrick came back from New York to help put his touches on the house, along with my cousin who was also a carpenter. Mike put a lot of sweat equity into the home too. He was Herb's subcontractor for years; he was the kind of guy who would drive my honey crazy. And as many times as they had a tiff, he always came back. During demo time, he smashed holes in the walls and climbed through the sheetrock to surprise Joey. We handed our five-year-old a hammer and let him join in on the fun! My brother and the crew he worked with hung the sheetrock, and an aunt of mine and her husband plastered. Many hands went into this renovation. And even though it didn't seem like much to brag about, we loved it there. It felt like we discovered a hidden treasure. In faith, we moved a lot of our belongings in totes (before winter) into the barn. I purchased a brand-new Jacuzzi tub from craigslist for $150, which also remained in the barn. The first to relocate were the chickens. We figured it might be easier when we were ready to sell the house we were still living in without them there. We put the house we were living in on the market. It would take us five months to sell.

Sadie (our dog) took a turn for the worse. She was losing weight and vomiting. I tried everything I could think of. I brought her to the vet up the road. He drew blood, and we learned she was suffering from kidney failure. I had a suspicion it had something to do with her dog food. Come to find out, there was a recall on the exact same brand of dog food we were feeding her. That angered me. In essence (unknowingly), I poisoned our pet. The food I offered her had high levels of vitamin D. I tried herbal remedies, but she was wasting away. Even though she still wagged her nubby tail, the life was disappearing in her eyes. I called the vet on a weekend and was so thankful he answered his phone. He told me even though he wasn't working that day, he would euthanize her and put her out of her misery. It was a few weeks before Christmas. A kind neighbor came over with his tractor and offered to bury her for us. That was the first time the boys lost a pet of their own. Our house was unusually quiet that week.

February 6, 2019, at 12:01 p.m. (the only reason I know this exactly is from reading an old text message)—it was a cold winter day, but the sun was shining. I just had a conversation over the phone with my sister hashing out my dilemma with her. Bundled up in my coat and scarf all alone, I had a fresh perspective. I noticed the barn and the "mystery" tree (we didn't know what it was, but we were hoping it was an apple tree) in the backyard. I looked down at the porch that was under my feet and noticed the platform was land level like I always envisioned. That was the moment I knew this was home. I burst into tears as I felt God's presence. He nudged my heart that I was exactly where I was meant to be. I immediately texted my honey with a picture of the view off the back porch. My text read:

> This is OUR HOME!!!! We're not getting robbed anymore, my love! Final decision!!!! You made this for us!!!! I love it here!!!!

His short but sweet response was, "Okay, sweetie. It's ours." The confirmation I was waiting for finally came. It didn't come from my sister, my children, my friends, my honey, or Harold and Jane Harper—it was a gentle whisper from the Holy Spirit. I needed to hear Him in stillness, in the quiet. I was overwhelmed with relief and joy.

Deeply Rooted

And now, just as you accepted Christ Jesus as your Lord, you must continue to follow him. Let your roots grow down into him, and let your lives be built on him. Then your faith will grow strong in the truth you were taught, and you will overflow with thankfulness.

—Colossians 2:6–7 NLT

The house was finally finished. After countless nights of whiting out blueprints, the idea became real and tangible! Maybe it wasn't love at first sight, but neither was the man God would give me as a partner for almost thirty years (for the record, my honey is not homely; all three of our boys get their handsome genes from him!). It's not about the exterior of something; it's about the heart, what's inside. Hence the popular maxim, "You can't judge a book by its cover."

This farm home was a labor of love. May 2, 2019, was move-in day! Twelve days later, the new owners moved into the house we moved out of. I asked Mike if he would take a couple pictures of me and the three boys carrying Herb over the threshold. What a keepsake!

Looks like Harold's prayer was answered. We live in the same town less than three miles down the road from him and his wife, Jane. I think he might have a prophetic gift he doesn't know about!

There's something familiar that can be seen from each house we've ever been in. The wide-planked pine floors that were installed reminded me of the southern yellow pine floors we originally put down at the Cape. The brick that Little Herbie helped mortar for the firewall and hearth was identical to the multiple times we installed them before (he did a great job, I might add!). Remember those mango walls? The same color radiates now in our living room. And the curtains that were left behind in our last house by the realtor adorned our windows. The gingham picture board that displayed a collage of portraits is hanging up in the hallway. The boys chose colors for their bedroom walls, *again*! We picked Rustic Alder cabinets in the kitchen with brushed copper knobs. Since we knew this was it, my honey remembered a table set my great-uncle Sonny made me and my sister when we were little. He transformed the bench into my kitchen island (Keri can keep the table). How could I not cry? The finishing touch was when my honey nailed in the post that had been marking all three of our sons' growth since they were old enough to stand. We pulled that piece of wood out from every single house and reinstalled it each time! I didn't want to lose those precious memories! And how could I forget—my dwarf apple tree could finally let her roots grow—it was symbolic—so could we.

For years, we collected *Mother Earth News* magazines and dreamt of building a home like the ones we would read about. Every other house we built usually had exterior vinyl siding; this time, we wanted wooden shiplap. We adjusted to a little more than half the square footage we were used to. Even though it wasn't a necessity, my honey added a front porch to the home (he knew how much I loved porches). Now Mimi had a beautiful covered porch by the entrance of her small abode. We hung up a tea-stained American flag, purple petunia baskets, and a white front-porch swing. It reminded me of a country store that you'd see back in the day. We also had the blessing of a back porch to overlook the view of the barn, our mystery tree, and the gardens. We knew until we could add a mudroom, we needed a place for muck boots to keep manure from being trudged through the house. Out of all the houses we ever lived in, this was the first one that had a barn.

When I unpacked our belongings from the totes, I was so thankful I didn't throw away the knickknack I bought in faith when we were trying to purchase the "decoy" property in Warren. This tiny box sign with white font reads, "Heaven's a little closer in the barn." Less than three weeks from moving in, we added three-day-old calves Moxie May (a black angus heifer) and Ruger Ray (a bull calf) to our homestead. We transported them in the back of the minivan! That was a memorable ride. The boys sported faces of wonder and laughter engulfed the vehicle while the calf was trying to lick them from the back seat.

Our hobby homestead welcomed forty-eight baby chicks, seven turkeys, and a small rat terrier puppy named "Tootsie." She is so small and adorable! As for Umi? She seems to enjoy her freedom. She used to be an indoor cat, but now she spends her days in the barn and comes in at night before bed. We've made maple syrup and homemade butter and ice cream from the raw milk we buy from a local dairy farm. The boys catch fireflies in mason jars and enjoy the occasional campfire.

My honey replied to an ad on craigslist again; this time, it was for several adult fruit trees. We always wanted a mini orchard, and the listing price was around three hundred dollars—good deal! When he came home with a flatbed of fruit trees, I was in awe. "Kristi, you're not gonna believe this!" he said.

"Believe what?"

"The man *gave* me all these fruit trees for *free*!"

"Seriously? No way! How come?"

"His family originally came from Russia years ago. He wanted these trees to go to good hands. During the revolt, his family wasn't able to bring many belongings with them, and being in such a hurry, they hid apple seeds with the few items they brought with them and relocated to Canada. When they moved to Worcester, Massachusetts, they transplanted the trees again. He and his wife are moving once more and just wanted the right person to have them."

Incredible! What an honor! I hope when we have a harvest, we will find that man, tell him the trees are safe and sound, and bless him with a bushel! The heavens opened up that day, and all night my honey felt the importance of making sure each tree was safely put back into the soil.

I struggled a bit but managed to hang the tire swing for the last time onto our mystery tree. And since it was spring, I was delighted to find crocus and daffodils sprouting from the earth. Like the joy of a child on Christmas Day opening presents, I would walk around with my cup of coffee in the mornings to find new life on the lilac bushes. A kind neighbor welcomed us to the neighborhood with a few plants; she has a vineyard up the street. I assumed she would know what the beautiful coral-pinkish bush was that was in the front of our yard. I was right; she called it a flowering quince. We had ornamental yellow forsythia, a weeping cherry tree, purple iris, and wild morning glories!

One of my favorite fragrances came from the back of the property. I followed the aroma to a honeysuckle bush tucked near the pines. We also found a peach tree that was budding too! Someone else took the time to sow love into this land. Appreciatively, we were blessed to reap the fruits of their labor. Later in the season, I discovered peonies, azaleas, and a bleeding heart!

You won't believe what that mystery tree was. Even though it had been neglected, unpruned, and appeared dead (I remembered when my honey suggested we should just cut it down that fall, but I asked him to wait and see if it was still alive in the spring)—we were pleasantly surprised. There were thousands of apple blossoms proudly boasting their splendor. Clusters of pinkish-white flowers were everywhere! She looked like a tree that belonged in the Garden of Eden. It was absolutely *magical* and breathtaking! I was so overjoyed. Only God knows the true desires of our heart. I don't second- or triple-guess anymore; I just know this is where we belong. It's our small piece of heaven on earth.

It felt so good to be home. On a warm sunny day, we held a cremation ceremony over the BBQ. For years, I used to wear this tank top that had the words "Always Moving." The words were meant to be exercise-related, but it toyed with me! We rebuked that shirt! Our family stood around the fire, said a prayer, and watched as my honey doused that shirt with lighter fluid and burned it to ashes. That felt so liberating!

My honey had a sign erected on the front of the barn. It took us a great deal of time to finally decide the name of our farm; it had to be meaningful. DEEPLY ROOTED FAMILY FARM was born! In bold letters, we admired the sign as it hung with the scripture reference: Colossians 2:6–7, established 2019.

What's the best way to give God glory for all He has done for us? What's a great way to share our victory and celebrate? That's right, you read my mind! A hootenanny! One sunny late summer day, we invited friends, family, and church family to a fun-filled gathering. Auntie Manda, Uncle Sam, and Alleigh came down from Vermont for the weekend and helped us prepare for the special day. One of the team leaders from the boys' ministry is also a chef; he cooked a Southern-style buffet: corn bread, bean and potato salad, pulled pork, and dirty rice. Yum! I made a cake for dessert that had a white fence, a red barn, a couple cows, baby chicks, a red tractor, a gray cat, and a small black dog (just like Tootsie). The black icing read, "Thank You, Jesus!"

We placed bales of hay around the backyard for some seating, bought a huge red tent, and filled a watering trough with ice. Prizes were to be won for the potato-sack races and the pie-eating contest. Mike got first place. Maggie the clown made balloon animals for the kids and face-painted. We rented a snow-cone machine, put up an old-fashioned lemonade stand, a self-serve candy-apple station, and a selfie station with hilarious props. The picture frame for the selfie was an old rusty door to a 1930s Model A pickup truck. Some of the props to choose from were overalls, mustaches, disposable hillbilly teeth, suspenders, cowboy hats, an old granny wig, a dress, and a pitchfork.

It wouldn't be a hootenanny without music! Erika, Dustin, and I sang a playlist of country, gospel, and Christian music. And Joey (only five years old) grabbed the microphone and gave his best version of "You Are My Sunshine." Erika's friend Billy knew a sound guy and invited another talented man who knew how to drum a cajón. Evans and Jack from church played guitar. You know me, obsessed with details. I even found a cute shirt that matched our red-and-white checkered tablecloths. It went well with a pair of denim jeans and the cowboy boots I begged my honey to buy me from Cracker Barrel.

Decorations were simple: red-and-white polka-dotted bloomers and men's white crew socks hung from a clothesline along with red-and-white balloons filled with helium. With chalk-colored ink on black posters, we thanked Jesus and all who played a part in help-ing us finally achieve our dream. We wanted to sincerely acknowl-edge that if not for the love, support, and help of others, it would have never been possible. One among many special moments for me that day was when we were giving Harold and Jane the grand tour. Harold told me he's never seen me so happy. Jane mentioned to Harold, "Can you believe we almost talked them out of this?" It was important to me for them to see what we were chasing. It wasn't a vapor in the wind. It was a promise from God Himself.

If you're wondering what happened to the historical colonial, it sold before Christmas that year to a family who interestingly wasn't "looking" for a house. They stumbled upon it and fell in love. It took faith for them to put an offer in. We accepted their offer even though there was a contingency for their house to sell in Spencer. That couple seemed to be a lot like us. We prayed God would sell it for them; we wanted people who would appreciate that home to have it. We always gift a Bible to the new owners of every home we flip. This one was extraspecial to us. We were inspired by the movie *It's a Wonderful Life* to bless them with a note that explained the items in their basket: "Here is bread that this house may never know hunger, salt that life may always have flavor, and wine that joy and prosperity may reign forever!"

You should have seen the abundance of apples we got our first year from that one tree. We filled totes, and I made homemade apple-sauce. We're still learning a lot. Now we have three pigs (Moe, Larry, and Curly) and two new calves (Ferdinand and Guapo). (If you're a vegetarian, please don't ask me where Moxie and Ruger went.) More chicks came in a couple weeks ago; maybe someday we will try to incubate them on our own again.

I'm no expert, but through my experience, I've learned a few things along the way. Life isn't fair, and it certainly hasn't been easy. Sometimes I'm broken, and I get discouraged. Sometimes before God can use me, He empties haughtiness out so when He pours in humility, there's enough room! I've learned to be open for correc-tion, to speak life, to say "I'm sorry," to pray a lot, to be still, to find true joy, to be thankful, to help others, to forgive (not frugally), to